The Church in our Times

RUPERT E. DAVIES

The Church in our Times

*An ecumenical history
from a British perspective*

WIPF & STOCK · Eugene, Oregon

Wipf and Stock Publishers
199 W 8th Ave, Suite 3
Eugene, OR 97401

The Church in our times
An Ecumenical History from a British Perspective
By Davies, Rupert E.
Copyright©1979 Methodist Publishing - Epworth Press
ISBN 13: 978-1-5326-3169-6
Publication date 4/25/2017
Previously published by Epworth Press, 1979

Every effort has been made to trace the current copyright
owner of this publication but without success. If you have
any information or interest in the copyright, please contact the publishers.

*To my daughter Mary Sullivan
who may find it useful*

CONTENTS

Preface	9
1 Deep Divisions	11
2 The Denominations Carry On	23
3 The Growth of the Ecumenical Idea	38
4 Advances and Rebuffs 1945–60	48
5 The World is the Scene	60
6 The Church of Rome Renewed	75
7 Uncertain Britain in the Sixties	91
8 Hope Awaiting Fulfilment	108
Epilogue	123
Suggested further reading	127
Index	129

PREFACE

ALL HISTORY, as we now know, is written from a point of view, disclosed or undisclosed. I disclose what was mine in writing this book. I am deeply convinced that the Church of Jesus Christ is one Church by the will of God, and that the divisions in its visible structure and in its inward life are man-made. Therefore I hold that an essential element in the historical judgement to be passed on any assembly of Christians is its intention, or lack of intention, to heal these divisions.

For an author to have been an eye witness of the events which he describes has certain disadvantages for the reader, since what he reads is bound to be in some sense a personal account. Yet the advantages may well outweigh the disadvantages. In any case it is right that the reader should know that I took a personal, and often an active part in many of the events described in this book—notably in the second half of the Anglican–Methodist Conversations, in the Faith and Order Conferences of the World Council of Churches from Lund in 1952 to Accra in 1974, in the Uppsala Assembly of the World Council of Churches in 1968, in the revision of liturgy carried out by the Methodist Church in Great Britain, and in the inauguration of the Church of North India, as well as in the internal business of the Methodist Church in various capacities.

I owe a great debt to many of my friends, most of whom do not even know that I have been writing this book, for helping me to form the ideas which I here express, without, of course, holding any responsibility for what I say. I am especially grateful to Raymond George, Kenneth Greet, Harold Roberts, David Stacey, John Stacey, Gordon Wakefield, Kenneth Wilson and Pauline Webb, of the Methodist

Church; to Bishop F. A. Cockin (now deceased), Christian Howard, Basil Moss, Peter Morgan, James Packer, Richard Stewart, Bishop Robert Stopford (now deceased), John Todd, Bishop Oliver Tomkins, Lukas Vischer and Henry Wansbrough, of many other Churches; to my wife Margaret, who patiently endured my ecumenical travelling, discussed nearly every issue with me, and has a probably unrivalled knowledge of the practical working of local ecumenism; to Mary Tanner, of the Faith and Order Commission of the World Council of Churches, for her very careful and expert reading and re-reading of the whole, and for countless invaluable suggestions; and to Ann Weeks, of Nailsea, who has once again typed out the illegible.

Bishopsworth   RUPERT E. DAVIES
Bristol

July 1978

CHAPTER ONE

Deep Divisions

WHETHER the twentieth century began on January 1st 1900, or (as is more logically contended) on January 1st 1901, the turning of the century had little immediate effect on British life, and most things went on as before. But change in social and political affairs was on the way. Queen Victoria died early in 1901, and before the nine years' reign of Edward VII was over an entirely new direction of affairs was apparent. The growing military and naval strength of Russia and Germany had driven the country into a series of new alliances designed to preserve the *status quo* in Europe and the Far East. The treaties with Japan held back the Russians in their drive to the East, and the agreement with France was intended to be a warning to Germany. Yet a dangerous tension was building up in Europe, though the signs of this were appreciated only by the few.

At home, the Boer War, which took an unexpectedly long time to win, had divided the nation; the issue of Tariff Reform divided the dominant Tory Party, and the education controversy of 1902 and the succeeding years made the Tory Government less popular than ever. In 1906 the Liberals came into power with the biggest, and perhaps the last, majority in their history, and social reform became the order of the day. It was opposed by the House of Lords, and the long struggle to curtail the powers of that House dimmed the public awareness of the fact that the introduction by the Liberal Chancellor of the Exchequer, Lloyd George, of Old Age Pensions, increased taxes (to pay for the pensions), and insurance against sickness and unemployment, was beginning to change the social and economic structure of the nation.

Meanwhile, at the end of Edward's reign, and the start of George V's, the Trade Unions were conducting their arduous but successful campaign for legal recognition. Simultaneously the demand for Irish Home Rule was reaching, not for the first or last time, a boiling point; in fact, it was only the outbreak of the World War that took it off the boil and prevented a devastating civil war in Ireland.

But these exciting events did not disturb the even tenor of the Churches' way. It may well be the case that the peak of church attendance in this country had already been reached and passed, but this was apparent to no one. Each denomination was in effective control of its own people; the Church of England could answer for rather more than half of the church-going population, the other churches and the sects for the rest. The working classes, which were than still easily distinguishable from the rest of the population, were conspicuously absent from church services, except in rural areas and those parts of the towns where there was a Roman Catholic population or where the Salvation Army or the Primitive Methodists had gained some hold on their allegiance; but then they had never attended church very much at any time, and their absence did not worry the largely middle-class congregations of the faithful.

The rift between Anglicans and Free Churchmen (as they preferred, and prefer, to be called; 'Nonconformists' as others usually called them) remained absolute and unquestioned, and seemed to be permanent. Each Church pursued its own aims and formulated its own policy irrespectively of the others, apart from a limited amount of co-operation between the major Free Churches, chiefly the Methodists, the Baptists and the Congregationalists. The difference between 'Church' and 'Chapel' was rooted in history, going back to the Civil Wars, the Protectorate, and the Act of Uniformity of 1662; the effect of the last of these was to degrade 'Nonconformists' to the level of second-class citizens, without the right to public office or to a University education—a state from which they had gradually emerged, but not completely, and not without a sense of grievance and a deep consciousness of being looked down upon.

There was a social and cultural difference also, in that to belong to the Church of England by law established, entailed

DEEP DIVISIONS

a virtual monopoly in respect of higher appointments in government and education; and the culturally and socially superior classes, including the inheritors of the wealth that comes from the land, were firmly imbedded in a position of privilege. The results were that in the countryside the squire and the parson reigned supreme, and in the towns social prestige remained with the Anglicans, though wealth no longer belonged exclusively to them; and that Free Churchmen who had been successful in business, manufacturing and trade sometimes transferred their spiritual allegiance to the Church of England for largely social purposes.

At the other end of the social scale agricultural labourers were often Methodists of one kind or another, and so were many of the shopkeepers in villages and towns. The urban Free Churchmen of all kinds came from the owners of small businesses and the rest of the *petite bourgeoisie*, with an increasing number of elementary school teachers. As the century proceeded more Free Churchmen took advantage of the University education that had been opened to them since 1870 (though the numbers involved did not reach anything like a flood until after the Second World War), and this created larger social opportunities, while the Free Churches' emphasis on thrift, hard work and temperance (in the narrow sense) brought a fair number of their members to high positions in the business and municipal world, and incidentally made available from their pockets the funds without which a Free Church (especially) cannot continue.

If a rough generalization is permissible, Primitive and United Methodists and Baptists were skilled and unskilled manual workers, and often local Trade Union leaders and foremen; those in small business, education and the less exalted professions were Congregationalists and Wesleyan Methodists.

The difference was also, of course, theological. Anglicans, Methodists, Baptists, Congregationalists and Presbyterians all claimed to be strictly orthodox and to adhere to the Scriptural Faith which goes back to the Apostles. But there were manifest Free Church differences from Anglicanism in liturgical practice, sacramental thinking and doctrines of the priesthood and the ministry, as well as in the place occupied by the laity, in the teaching and preaching, and in the worship and administration of the Church. Yet there were differences also between the Free Churches themselves on the doctrines of the Church, the Ministry and the Sacraments, and the Wesleyan Methodists were theologically nearer to the Church of England than to the Baptists. It is hard to deny that theological differences between Church and Chapel were sometimes a cover for deeper differences in culture and psychology.

In the Church of England, its well-attached services and secure position did not conceal the serious conflicts within its own ranks—conflicts continued from the old century into the new. Most bitter of all was the conflict about ritualism: the descendants of the Tractarians had introduced into the parish churches certain practices which showed greater affinities to Rome than to the sobriety of the Book of Common Prayer, and were, in fact, contrary to 'lawful authority' as it was usually understood. Reservation of the sacrament on the High Altar, Benediction (the blessing of the people with the Host), the regular use of the Latin Missal and Corpus Christi processions through the streets were only some of the practices which did not square with the ordinary Englishman's conception of the National Church, and to the convinced Protestant were an abomination and a lie.

The Church Association, on behalf of the Evangelicals in the Church of England who wished to preserve the spirit of Protestantism, adopted exactly the procedure for combating 'Popery' which was best calculated to strengthen it. Its prosecution in 1888 of Bishop Edward King of Lincoln, a saintly and much-loved man, before the Archbishop of Canterbury, had aroused disgust rather than support among nonpartisans, but, undeterred, it went on to further prosecutions and to organized hooliganism and the disruption of public worship; one of the principal protesters and disrupters, John Kensit, was killed in a resultant riot in 1902. So there were martyrs on both sides, and no success for either. The Bishops seemed to be powerless, but good order of a kind was restored in 1905 by the report of a Royal Commission, which recom-

DEEP DIVISIONS

mended the condemnation of certain suspect practices such as Reservation and Benediction (though not of others), and the revision of the Church's laws about ornaments and vestments. As a more important consequence of the previous tumults and the coming of an uneasy peace, the revision of the Book of Common Prayer began to be seriously considered.

The Modernist controversy was also a continuation from the nineteenth century. Charles Gore, a greatly honoured leader among the Anglo-Catholics, had recommended in *Lux Mundi* in 1888 the acceptance of the results of Biblical Criticism that were solidly grounded. This caused a storm in conservative circles, but there were others in which he was thought to have gone not nearly far enough forward. Twenty years later the great majority of scholars and well-informed churchmen (though there were exceptions, as there still are) had come to acknowledge that it was no longer possible to believe every word of the Bible. But much more serious questions were now being raised, about the Virgin Birth, the miracles, the Resurrection, and the deity of Christ. *The New Theology* of R. J. Campbell (at first a Congregationalist, later an Anglican) suggested that Christ's person was divine because he was 'the supreme example of God's indwelling' in man; other teachers, following Adolf Harnack's *What is Christianity?* virtually reduced the Faith to belief in the fatherhood of God and the brotherhood of man, with a special place in the system for Jesus as a unique teacher and a superb human being in tune with God's purposes. In 1912 a group of Oxford men, most of whom later became bishops, brought out *Foundations*, which seemed to many at the time to be unpleasantly heterodox, but now would rank as extremely mild. In this B. H. Streeter argued that the resurrection of Christ was not physical but spiritual, and William Temple declared that the Chalcedonian Definition of 451, asserting two natures and one person of Christ, is, in fact, 'a confession of the bankruptcy of Greek patristic theology' (thus anticipating by 65 years some of the main contentions of the 1977 book, *The Myth of God Incarnate*).

In 1917 the British nation diverted some of its attention from the incessant horrors of the First World War (as it had done in 1915 to follow the intricacies of the 'brides in the bath' murders case) to observing the attempts of traditionalists, egged on by the *Church Times*, to prevent the consecration of Hensley Henson as Bishop of Hereford, on the ground of his alleged modernism. He was opposed also because he had preached in a Congregational Church, then a serious offence. He agreed to affirm the faith of the Creeds, and his consecration took place. Henson was not so much a modernist as a stalwart and highly articulate representative of the Broad Church tradition which goes back to the eighteenth century—the tradition according to which the general principles of the Creeds and the Prayer Book are to be adhered to without dogmatism and without excess of zeal or elaboration of ceremony.

Perhaps the Church of England would have fallen apart on these issues (yet this danger is often mentioned, but does not materialize) if it had not been for the patient statesmanship of Randall Davidson, who began twenty-five years as Archbishop of Canterbury in 1903. He was a man of peace, and of studious moderation, willing to listen to the exponents, however extravagant, of every view on every question, and particularly skilful at maintaining personal relationships between deep-dyed opponents.

The Free Churches entered the twentieth century in a state of greater complacency and also of greater harmony than they had previously exhibited. The largest of them, the Wesleyan Methodists, had never lost, and were later to revive, the desire for reunion with the Church of England; but they had, almost against their will, been induced by what seemed to be the growing Romanism of the Church of England to throw in their lot with the 'Old Dissent' of the Congregationalists and Baptists, and temporarily to become assimilated to it in its anti-sacramental outlook. The other Methodist Churches tended towards Dissent in any case. The Methodist leader nearest to the other Free Churches was Hugh Price Hughes, who was a disciple of F. D. Maurice, and through his preaching, and his editorship of the *Methodist Times*, inspired many Free Churchmen with a concern for social justice and zeal for the Liberal Party. He died, prematurely, in 1920, but not before he had conceived, and begun to carry out, a plan for establishing Wesleyan Methodist 'Central Halls' in all the main cities, to minister to both the spiritual and the physical needs of their down-town areas.

His successor in many fields was John Scott Lidgett, who was born in 1854 and worked on through almost ten decades. Lidgett was notable for, among other things, his theological writings in the tradition of F. D. Maurice, the community work in Bermondsey which was focused in the Settlement which he founded, and his contribution to national education at many levels.

In isolation from each other, therefore, the Churches and their leaders were no doubt very busy. But their position in society was so much taken for granted and so easy to maintain that preoccupation with their own affairs seemed neither unnatural nor wrong. The penalty of ecclesiastical success and large congregations was the absence of any incentive to probe at all deeply the new problems of contemporary society. Inherited answers, attitudes and practices seemed to most Christians to be wholly adequate to the present and the future; self-questioning and self-criticism did not appear on their programme.

There was one matter on which the Church of England and the Free Churches were forced by circumstances to meet together. And when they did so, it was in angry confrontation. The education of the people was the battleground.

The progress of popular education had been hampered and bedevilled for many years by the rivalry between the National Society (which promoted Anglican Schools) and the British and Foreign Society (which promoted Free Church Schools); this was a pity and a shame, not least because the Churches had initiated popular education in the first place. With the advent of local School Boards, empowered to set up and maintain elementary schools for the children not catered for by the denominational Societies, most Free Churchmen decided that the time had come to scrap denominational schools altogether, to pay for all schools with the rates and to include undenominational religious teaching in the curriculum. So the Schools of the British and Foreign Society

17

ceased gradually to exist. Sir Robert Morant's Bill of 1902, put forward on behalf of the Conservative Government, went the opposite way; the School Boards were to be scrapped; newly created Local Education Authorities were to support both denominational and other schools with the rates, and leave the arrangement of religious instruction to the managers of the schools, on the old denominational lines where Church Schools were concerned; they were also to provide secondary and higher education for the first time.

The Bill was in many respects progressive and far-seeing, but the proposal to support Church Schools with the rates roused the ire of most Free Churchmen to an explosive level. It was pointed out that about a million Free Church children in Anglican Schools, usually the only schools available in the neighbourhood, would either have to make themselves conspicuous by withdrawl from religious instruction (which was allowable under the Cowper-Temple Clause), or be subjected to Anglican proselytization. This was, in the climate of the times, a fearful prospect, and John Clifford, the Baptist, led a movement of Passive Resisters, pledged to withhold the payment of rates and to go to prison if necessary. Many Methodists, including their chief education adviser, Scott Lidgett, were not whole-heartedly in favour of Dr Clifford's protest, seeing the good elements in the Bill, and willing for the Dual System to continue for a little longer (as it still does).

The Bill passed into law in spite of the opposition, and the Liberals promised to repeal it when they came to power. They duly drafted a new Bill in 1906, transferring the Church Schools to the Local Education Authorities. At this point the Roman Catholics and the Anglicans, with the backing of the House of Lords, provided the angry opposition, and in spite of attempts by Scott Lidgett and others to arrange a compromise, the Bill was dropped, leaving many hard feelings behind.

Both the nature and the results of the education controversy showed how deep was the mutual suspicion of the Churches. Church and Chapel stood embattled against each other. But there were a few people who had begun to see the deep disgrace of this situation. Henry Lunn, of travel agency fame and wealth had, in 1892, invited the whole bench of

Anglican bishops, the leaders of all the other British Churches, and Mr Gladstone, to a conference at Grindelwald. Useful conversations were held (in the absence of Mr Gladstone, who had other duties), but they made it clear that the time for rapprochement between Anglicans and Free Churchmen had not yet come. Yet a much greater degree of Free Church co-operation than in the past did begin to take place as a result of these conversations. In 1896 the National Council of Evangelical Free Churches had been founded. This was not a fully representative body, and did not satisfy those who wished to press on to a United Free Church. One of these, and the most enthusiastic, was J. H. Shakespeare, Secretary of the Baptist Union, and his efforts resulted in 1919 in the formation of the Federal Council of Evangelical Free Churches, which succeeded in being a body representative of Congregationalists, Baptists, Presbyterians and the various kinds of Methodists. But there was little progress towards a United Free Church, partly because the Wesleyan Methodist Church still wished to keep open the door to reunion with the Church of England.

Scott Lidgett led the Wesleyan Methodists in this matter also. He based his appeal for reunion on Biblical and theological principles, many of them derived from the Epistle to the Ephesians (thus giving the lie to those who say that the campaign to reunite the Church is just the desperate effort of declining communities to keep themselves alive). He declared to the Wesleyan Methodist Conference in 1908 that the time had come to reconcile the witness of the various Churches in the larger synthesis of a reasonable faith which holds together the contentions of the separated Churches.

This was two years before the event which is usually regarded as the start of the Ecumenical Movement, the Missionary Conference at Edinburgh in 1910. This had been called for by a meeting in New York of non-Anglican missionary societies in 1900, still more by the obvious fact that missionaries of various denominations in various countries were hampered by foolish overlapping and competition, and not a little by the increasing recognition of Biblical scholars of all denominations that the New Testament posits one Gospel and one Church. The Missionary Societies worked together with a will to call the Conference. They easily persuaded the Student Christian Movement, then a predominantly missionary body, to service the conference that was being arranged. Then they set about persuading Archbishop Randall Davidson to give the occasion his blessing and his presence. He was reluctant at first, since the Anglo-Catholics among his advisers feared that this was to be a Protestant gathering, but in the end he agreed, and his agreement brought in the Churches of the Anglican Communion and their Missionary Societies, such as the Society for the Propagation of the Gospel, which had at first held back. Rome, of course, was not represented—the time for this was in the distant future.

John R. Mott, the American Methodist, was the Chairman, J. H. Oldham, the Anglican layman, was the Secretary, and the young William Temple was an usher in the gallery. The Conference discussed the missionary message, and found that it was shared by all the Societies; missionary strategy, which needed and received a good deal of rationalization; the training of missionaries; the relation of the missionary churches to the governments of their countries; and the place of African and Asian nationals in their own Churches. The need to discuss this last point was emphasized by the fact that only 2 per cent of those present were non-missionaries and non-white, and by the immensely impressive speech of Azariah, later Bishop of Dornakal, the first non-white to become a bishop in the Anglican Communion.

The immediate result of Edinburgh was the International Missionary Council, the further result was the Faith and Order Movement, which will be more fully described in later pages; and the long term results were the gradual and steady growth of understanding among the Churches from then until today.

A probably unwise expression of the Edinburgh spirit took place in Kikuyu, East Africa, in 1913. The non-Roman Catholic missions there considered a scheme of federation on the basis of the Bible, the Creeds and the Gospel Sacraments, without any mention of episcopacy, and proposed full intercommunion on this basis. The news of this when it reached England created a loud furore, which was made the more strident by the excommunication of the two bishops who had been present by the Bishop of Zanzibar. Undoubtedly the action of the conference was excellently meant but premature, and the echoes of the conflict did not die away until war with Germany broke out on August 4th 1914. This early ecumenism, and even Edinburgh itself, were the concern of a few individuals and groups with ideas and vision beyond their time. Yet by hindsight we can see that it offered vast promise for the future, far greater than anyone then dared to hope.

It could scarcely be expected that the Churches, so set in their ways, so complacent and so deeply separated from each other, would be able to give a spiritual, ethical or intellectual lead to the nation during the shattering experience of the 1914–18 war. Nor did they give such a lead. But it has to be acknowledged that the world and the nation had entered suddenly into an unprecedented situation for which any preparations would have been inadequate. At the beginning, when the air was filled with stories of German atrocities in Belgium (and of Russian soldiers marching through London with snow on their boots), the pulpits resounded with calls to arms against the Kaiser, thought of as the Devil Incarnate. As the war in the west settled down to multiplied pointless slaughter, ministers and clergy at home had their time filled with comforting the bereaved and upholding civilian morale, while chaplains on the field were busy both with these and with even more gruesome tasks. There also emerged in idealistic circles, as a counterblast to the bitter cynicism of many, a kind of patriotic mysticism flavoured with Christianity, and expressed in the hymn which was published in 1919 and sung on many Remembrance Days for years to come:

> O valiant hearts, who to your glory came
> Through dust of conflict and through battle flame;
> Tranquil you lie, your knightly virtue proved,
> Your memory hallowed in the land you loved.
>
> Splendid you passed, the great surrender made,
> Into the light that never more shall fade;
> Deep your contentment in that blest abode,
> Who wait the last clear trumpet-call of God.

THE CHURCH IN OUR TIMES

> Long years ago, as earth lay dark and still,
> Rose a loud cry upon a lonely hill,
> While in the frailty of our human clay
> Christ, our redeemer, passed the self-same way.
>
> These were his servants, in his steps they trod,
> Following through death the martyred Son of God.
> Victor he rose; victorious too shall rise
> They who have drunk his cup of sacrifice.

Such sentiments, and the salutation of all the fallen in battle as Christian martyrs, did not survive the twenties and thirties, and were rarely asserted in the Second World War. But they were sincerely held at the time.

There were, of course, Christian conscientious objectors, but the theology of pacifism had not been expounded or grasped, and they received short shrift, as little better than traitors, from Church as well as State. But there were also a few Christians who accepted both the grim necessity and the awfulness of war, and planned to build a Christian Commonwealth out of the ruin, the sacrifices, the courage and the fellowship of war. Among them were G. A. Studdert-Kennedy ('Woodbine Willie' to the troops) who by his understanding of men and his appeal to their deepest qualities became the army chaplain *par excellence*, and after the war founded the Industrial Christian Fellowship to further his aims; and T. B. ('Tubby') Clayton, who turned the soldiers' club, Talbot House, at Poperinghe near Ypres, into a Christian community centre for officers and men, with its own ceremony of 'the lighting of the lamp'. After the war he founded Toc H (as the signallers pronounced the signal T H) to bring together men and women of all denominations, ranks, classes and political views for service to the community.

Some good, then came out of the evil of war; and many servicemen and civilians dreamed of making post-war Britain 'a land fit for heroes to live in'. Disappointment was to follow. And for that disappointment disunited Christians must bear their share of the blame; though the politicians and the public must also shoulder theirs.

CHAPTER TWO

The Denominations Carry On

AT THE END of 1918 the British nation began to turn from the miseries of war to face the dangers of peace. These were to include the Treaty of Versailles, the General Strike, the Great Depression and mass unemployment, the rise of Hitler and the rearmament of Germany, the Abdication, the Spanish Civil War, the Berlin–Rome Axis, the Munich Agreement and the stirring up of these ingredients into the Second World War. In fact it has been suggested, half seriously, that we ought to speak not of *two* World Wars, but of only one, with a period of comparative quiescence between 1918 and 1938.

It was thus a formidable world and a deeply troubled society in which the Churches had to operate. Their human resources were smaller than they themselves suspected, and grew smaller still throughout the twenty years to 1939. Many of those who had fought in the trenches and elsewhere came home deeply disillusioned with what they called 'organized religion', and often with Christianity itself. The Churches, in their judgement, had signally failed, not only to stop the war and the resultant atrocities and corruptions, but also to deal with the deep issues of faith and conduct that the cataclysmic conflict had raised. Why were both sides convinced that God was on their side? No reply. Why were no one's prayers for peace answered for four years? No reply. Why did God allow the senseless destruction of millions of human lives? No reply.

The gaps in church congregations were largely due, of course, to the length of the casualty lists; but the disillusionment of ex-Servicemen explained many others, and those who continued to attend church often did so only out of a sense of duty and family feeling. Thus the Churches had suffered a great inner impoverishment, though the results of this were slow to appear.

In this condition they were particularly vulnerable to the assaults of the twentieth-century rationalists who flourished in the twenties and thirties. Bertrand Russell allied his great prestige as a mathematician and a mathematical philosopher to the cause of an atheism which was not new but was in his case beautifully argued. He also anticipated the permissive society of several decades later by advocating trial marriages, and declaring that the sexual act was no more significant than drinking a glass of water when one is thirsty. Lytton Strachey reinforced the fashionable school of 'de-bunking' historians by showing in *Eminent Victorians* that the much-vaunted piety of certain nineteenth-century heroes was a sham. H. G. Wells used his knowledge of modern science to raise hopes (which he later himself abandoned) of a technological utopia which could dispense with God, and Bernard Shaw (quoting Nietzsche) declared that there had been only one Christian ever, and he had been crucified—though he partly retracted that view by his sympathetic portrayal of the Maid of Orleans in his famous play about her. The Bloomsbury Set, to which some of these authors belonged, put about the notion that Christianity was intellectually disreputable, and Virginia Woolf took it as an act of personal betrayal when T. S. Eliot, one of its members, became a Christian.

In spite of their inability to deal successfully with these challenges the Churches succeeded in making some impact on public affairs. They threw their influence behind the activities of the League of Nations until that body crumbled under the weight of the European dictators. Archbishop Randall Davidson took strenuous measures to stop the Coal Strike in 1926, though without success. Churches of many denominations (the Methodists in the Rhondda Valley were a notable example) did all they could to alleviate the hardships of unemployment when the State did little and even reduced such unemployment benefit as there was. Archbishop Lang, who succeeded Archbishop Davidson in 1928, was a major moral and personal influence in bringing about the abdication of Edward VIII. Not all these interventions were well-judged, but they at least showed a continuing sense of responsibility for the life of the nation.

THE DENOMINATIONS CARRY ON

But for the most part each of the Churches pursued its own concerns. In 1919 the Archbishops called the Church of England to a 'National Mission of Repentance and Hope', based on the parishes. But repentance was not widely held to be necessary, as the war had just been won, the other Churches were not involved, and party strife in the Church of England greatly weakened the force of the Mission. Bishop Hensley Henson acidly remarked that the slump in religion had not been arrested.

Much more significant for the Church of England was the 'Life and Liberty Movement'. The 'liberty' aimed at was freedom, or relative freedom, from dependence on Parliament, which, as matters stood, had to be persuaded to pass a Bill for any major change in the life of the Church, such as the creation of a new parish, to be effected. The vigorous advocacy of the Movement by the younger generation of Church leaders, notably William Temple and H. R. L. Sheppard, brought reform on to the statute book. The Enabling Act of 1919 created the Church Assembly by combining the Convocations (of clergy only) with a stated number of laymen, and set up Parochial Church Councils, elected by those baptized in the Church of England and not belonging to another Church. Thus Anglican laity were given a greater say in parish affairs, though they still had much less than in the Free Churches.

The Church Assembly was authorized by the Enabling Act to enact legislation on certain matters, and 'lay it on the table' of the Houses of Parliament; if it was not challenged within thirty days it became the law of the land and of the Church. This applied, among other things, to proposals for altering the Church's worship, and was brought into operation when at last a revised Book of Common Prayer was approved by the Assembly in 1927.

It had taken 25 years to reach this point. The Evangelical party desired no change in the Prayer Book; the Anglo-Catholics wanted full legal recognition of practices, such as the continuous reservation of the sacrament, which their convictions impelled them to carry out illegally. Those in the middle wished certain services to be improved in language

25

THE CHURCH IN OUR TIMES

and tone, and were willing for some Anglo-Catholic practices to be legitimized if only it would bring peace to the Church. In the end 39 out of 43 bishops agreed to the proposed revisions, which included the amendment of the Order of Holy Communion to include the Invocation of the Holy Spirit, authorization to reserve (but not to adore) the Sacrament and some re-writing of prayers and services. Large majorities in the courts of the Church followed the bishops' lead.

The Prayer Book Measure was laid on the table of both Houses of Parliament, and a debate was immediately demanded in both. The Lords approved the Measure without difficulty. Exactly how many practising Anglicans, non-practising Anglicans, Free Churchmen of various kinds, Roman Catholics, members of the Church of Scotland, agnostics and atheists made up the House of Commons is not known. But they all, of course, had an equal say and vote in the matter. After a stormy debate, With the British public showing a lively interest which nowadays would be inconceivable, the Measure was rejected by 238 votes to 205. One of the most powerful speeches against the Measure was made by a Scottish Presbyterian, Rosslyn Mitchell. The Measure was brought back to the House by the bishops a year later, and thrown out by a larger majority.

No doubt the vote reflected the latent fears of Popery (which was not really in question) still prevalent among Englishmen; no doubt Randall Davidson, who preferred the old Book of Common Prayer, did not give a strong enough lead; no doubt the non-Anglican Members of Parliament under the constitution had a perfect right to speak and vote (actually the majority of English M.P.s were in favour of the motion). But it was a clear case of the imposition of its will by a largely secular state on the Church of England at its most vital point, its worship.

No wonder there was a loud cry for disestablishment, uttered most clearly by Hensley Henson, who had previously been a State-and-Church man. If disestablishment had been carried through, the Church of England would have gained the spiritual freedom it does not even yet quite possess, and

THE DENOMINATIONS CARRY ON

subsequent union negotiations with other Churches would have been greatly eased. But the Church, in its own judgement, would have lost its moral influence on State affairs, and this it was not prepared to do. The movement for disestablishment gradually lost its impetus.

Randall Davidson retired soon after the rejection of the Prayer Book Measure. The biships decided to permit the use of the revised Prayer Book wherever the Parochial Church Council agreed. The use became widespread, but not universal. The revised book never really transferred the affections of Anglicans from the 1662 Book of Common Prayer, and the 1927 revisions have in any case been swept away by the new liturgical thought of recent years. The 1927 phraseology sounds strangely out-of-date today.

If the age just described was the age of Randall Davidson for the Church of England, the one that followed was the age of William Temple for the Church *in* England. It was he who decisively brought the Church of England out of its isolation; it was he who encouraged the Free Churches to come out of theirs. It was he who acquainted British Christians with the movements of thought and action in the world Church. It was he who provided a focus of unity for many disparate groups and parties in his own Church. He became, as very few have been since the Reformation, the Archbishop of the English people.

His academic prowess brought him a Fellowship in Philosophy at the Queen's College, Oxford, and the Headmastership of Repton School. But he became a better Bishop of Manchester than he had been a Headmaster, because he was most fully extended when he was in touch with all classes of the community, not just with one. Translated to York in 1928, he clearly exercised a greater influence on the country at large than his brother at Canterbury, and it was a matter of some consternation that Winston Churchill, when Archbishop Lang retired, delayed for so long Temple's inevitable appointment to succeed him—no doubt because of his left-wing tendencies. He did not live long enough to carry into effect the plans which he had conceived for Church and State after the Second World War: in particular, his death robbed

27

the Churches of the lead in matters ecumenical which he was already giving.

As a preacher and lecturer never at a loss for the right word or sentence, he exercised his profoundest influence on the young and lively-minded. The mission to the University of Oxford which he conducted in 1931 was a turning point in the lives of many men and women who might otherwise have fallen victims to the cynicism and scepticism which had been prevalent in the University since the end of the First World War.

As a thinker he belonged to the school of thought, now defunct, according to which God is the Absolute, the Being in whom thought and reality coincide. But he modified this view considerably to include the real humanity of Jesus, who, crucified, risen and ascended, now invited us to share with him the life of God by union with him in the sacrifice of Gethsemane and Calvary. In his later years he repudiated the last remnants of his earlier intellectualism by declaring that it is the task of the Christian, not only or chiefly to understand the world, but to change it. Certainly no one was ever less content than he to allow thought to remain abstract, no one more eager than he to translate it into loving action for human dignity and fulfilment.

The movement in the Church of England towards Christian unity was not initiated by him, though he became in the end the chief agent for carrying it on. The third Lambeth Conference of bishops of the Anglican Communion, meeting in 1888, had issued the Lambeth Quadrilateral, stating the four Anglican requirements for the reunion of the Churches. These were the acceptance by all parties of '(a) the Holy Scriptures of the Old and New Testaments, as "containing all things necessary to salvation", and as being the rule and ultimate standard of faith; (b) the Apostles' Creed as the Baptismal Symbol, and the Nicene Creed as the sufficient statement of the Christian Faith; (c) the two Sacraments ordained by Christ Himself—Baptism and the Supper of the Lord—ministered with unfailing use of Christ's Words of Institution, and of the elements ordained by Him; (d) the Historic Episcopate, locally adapted in the methods of its

THE DENOMINATIONS CARRY ON

administration to the varying needs of the nations and peoples called of God into the Unity of His Church'.

The issuing of the Quadrilateral did not in itself do much for the promotion of unity. But it was there to be taken up later and put to good use. When the bishops assembled at Lambeth for the Sixth Conference in 1920 they were presumably aware that in May of the year before, in Tranquebar in South India, thirty-three members of different denominations, mostly ministers, and nearly all Indian, had met to discuss means of ending the disunity which was damaging their work throughout South India. It seemed blasphemous and absurd to these Indian Christians that in the face of a predominantly non-Christian population and culture, the small group of Christians should be divided among themselves. At this conference at Tranquebar the idea of a 'Church of South India' was born. Negotiations began at once among Anglicans, Lutherans, Presbyterians and Congregationalists (the last two being already united in the South India United Church). Progress at first was very gradual, but it gained more momentum when the Methodists joined the negotiating group in 1925. The Edinburgh Conference in 1910 had laid down plans which led to the comity of missions, in accordance with which areas of the country were allotted each to a different denomination, to aviod apparent or real competition. But this had proved inadequate, and the Christan leaders of South India were convinced that the divinely intended solution was one Church, and for that end they were prepared to pray and work until it was accomplished.

Nearly all of this was in the future when the bishops came to Lambeth in 1920, but what they did when they arrived was an additional incentive to the activities in South India. For they issued an 'Appeal to all Christian People' to work for the visible unity of Christ's Church. Recognizing that the chief obstacle to such unity, in respect of theology, was the fact that while some believed in the necessity of the historic episcopate for valid ordinations to the ministry, and even for the existence of the Church, others did not, the bishops explicitly acknowledged in the Appeal 'all those who believe in our Lord Jesus Christ and have been baptized into the Name of

29

the Holy Trinity as sharing with them membership of the universal Church of Christ which is His Body'; and went on to assert that a united Church could be built only on the wholehearted acceptance of the Lambeth Quadrilateral, summed up as Scriptures, Creeds, the Sacraments instituted by Christ, and 'a ministry acknowledged by every part of the Church as possessing not only the inward call of the Spirit but also the commission of Christ and the authority of the Whole Body', with the added suggestion that the Historic Episcopate was the one and only means of providing such a ministry. Then it expressly disclaimed the intention of calling into question 'the spiritual reality' of non-episcopal ministries, which 'have been manifestly blessed and owned of the Holy Spirit as effective means of grace'.

The Appeal was warmly and gratefully received by the Free Churches of England and the Church of Scotland, and conversations between the Churches began which have, in a sense, continued to this day. The matters mentioned by the Appeal turned out, of course, to be not nearly so simple as they seem on first reading. Many interpretations are possible of such phrases as 'the spiritual reality of non-episcopal ministries' and 'affective means of grace'. But Free Churchmen can be forgiven if they think that the Church of England has sometimes, though not deliberately, gone back on the downright affirmations of the bishops in 1920; and indeed the equivalent pronouncement of the bishops in 1930, at the next Lambeth Conference, was not quite so forthcoming as that of 1920. But it can be replied that the 1920 Appeal was in no sense binding on the Church of England, for the Lambeth Conference is advisory, not authoritative. And indeed it seems to be true that the Appeal was well in advance of Anglican sentiment in this country then and perhaps, to some extent, is so still.

The first actual instance of a united church in the period after Lambeth was in Canada, but since the Anglican Church of Canada (not an 'established church', of course) did not share in it, it cannot be regarded as a direct result of the Lambeth Appeal. Presbyterians, Methodists and Congregationalists joined to form the United Church of Canada in 1925, on a non-episcopal basis. A not inconsiderable group of Presbyterians, however, as well as the Anglicans, abstained, and still abstain, from participation.

In the 1920s the various Methodist Churches of Great Britain were working strenuously towards union. In this case the Lambeth Appeal was more likely to be operative. For some of the leaders of the Wesleyan Methodist Church, notably Scott Lidgett, regarded Methodist Union as a step towards a larger unity, and saw to it that in the title deeds of the new Church provision was made for other unions if the Church decided to embark upon them.

Methodism had been grievously fissiparous in the nineteenth century. The Primitive Methodists were an early offshoot from the parent body, in 1807. But even before this there had been a smaller separation, and afterwards, especially during the middle part of the century, there were others, large and small. Nearly all the various separated groups, other than the Primitive Methodists, were combined in 1907 to form the United Methodist Church. Now it was a question of joining together the Wesleyan Methodists, the United Methodists and the Primitive Methodists. It cannot be said that ecumenical zeal was the sole factor in bringing the plan to a successful conclusion, for the two smaller Churches were in a state of comparative decline and their financial and other resources were stretched to the limit. But there was also a widespread conviction that division between those who professed loyalty to John Wesley, who was himself a man who regarded schism as one of the worst of sins, was no longer legitimate. The main opponents of the scheme were some Wesleyan Methodist ministers who feared that union with the more obviously 'non-conformist' bodies would jeopardize subsequent union with the Church of England, much as some Anglicans today fear that union with the Free Churches will jeopardize future union with Rome.

The union was consummated in 1932, and the first President of the Methodist Conference was, most appropriately, Scott Lidgett. The results of union were slow to appear in some parts of the country, and one can still hear talk of 'Prims' and 'Wesleyans' from time to time. But the generations which have arisen since the Second World War have resolutely turned their backs on past divisions, and simply regard themselves as Methodists. The Primitive and United Inheritance has continued in the united Church, not so much in the shape of leading personalities (though there have been some of these) as in the determination (not always successful) to give laypeople their proper place in the life of the Church, and in a certain suspicion in some quarters of the practices and beliefs of Anglicans.

Meanwhile, two other movements towards unity, less institutional, but not for that reason less effective in the long run, were gathering strength—'Faith and Order' and 'Life and Work'. The influence of William Temple was to be seen in both of them. Bishop Brent of the Philippines had been present at the Edinburgh Conference, and had observed that the participants had taken for granted throughout that they had the same Gospel to preach and the same mission to fulfil—and yet they were divided into different communions and could not take the Lord's Supper together. Surely there was something badly wrong here, something that required investigation, something that raised deep questions of faith and church order, and of the relation between them. So in his mind was formed the concept of a 'World Conference on Faith and Order' to which an invitation could be sent 'to all Christian bodies throughout the world which accept our Lord Jesus Christ as God and Saviour'. The World War greatly prolonged the time needed for the assembling of such a conference, but it took place in Lausanne in 1927, with about 400 delegates from over 100 churches. The Roman Catholic and Orthodox Churches were invited to send delegations, but felt unable to do so. The time of the Conference was largely spent in the statement of the various theological views of the main groups of Churches, leading to great astonishment on every hand at the discovery of how much they held in common; and the mere coming-together of people from different and apparently conflicting communions created an experience of spiritual fellowship which was the foundation stone of much that was to follow.

Outstanding delegates at the Lausanne Conference were William Temple and Nathan Söderblom, Archbishop of

Uppsala, and both of them were actively involved in another series of conferences that also stemmed from Edinburgh, 1910—this time on 'Life and Work', the application of the Christian message to the problems, national and international, of human society. The first conference with this title was held in Stockholm in 1925, and was closely linked in English minds with the Conference on Politics, Economics and Citizenship ('Copec') held in Birmingham in the year before, chaired by William Temple, prepared for by immense research on the problems discussed, and resulting in weighty volumes which have never been fully used.

Before 'Faith and Order' and 'Life and Work' could meet again on a world scale a dramatic change had come over the theological and the political scene in Europe. In the first decade after the War most teachers and preachers of influence in Europe and America had proclaimed a 'liberal' Gospel, emphasizing the humanity of Jesus, applying the category of progress to human nature and society, and to the revelation of truth to be found in the Bible, and directing the efforts of their disciples towards the creation of a war-free, humanitarian, democratic society of nations, which they identified with the Kingdom of God. But this version of Christianity came to ring less and less true in many parts of Europe, and especially in Germany, where there seemed to be no end to the aftermath of the war in the forms of political chaos, unemployment, disastrous inflation, and ultimately, armed gangs in the streets. Belief in progress and a world free from war struck most Germans, including many Christians, as an Anglo-Saxon pipe-dream born of political näiveté and ignorance of human nature.

So Christians in Germany, at least, were ready to welcome the 'crisis' theology of Karl Barth when it made its first impact in the early twenties, expressed with the measured eloquence of a preacher, the finely tempered acumen of a scholar, and the slightly obscure profundity of a Biblical prophet. Barth (1886-1968) was a Swiss, but he was a professor in Germany, until he was deprived of his Chair in Bonn by Hitler in 1935. He scorned the idea of progress in any form, least of all in religion, since man has no power whatever to know God or to improve himself or his lot; he set no store by religious experience. He had little use for Biblical criticism, though he did not entirely reject it; and none at all for philosophy as a preparation for Christian faith, or for any kind of natural theology. Christ, and Christ alone, is God's communication with man; he alone is the Word of God, in stark contrast to any word of man.

When Hitler came to power in 1933, he may have thought, if he considered the matter at all (which is unlikely), that Barth's influence would help to maintain the traditional abstinence of the Protestant Churches from participation in politics and from criticism of the current (or any) regime. Certainly the doctrine, derived from Martin Luther, and based on Romans XIII, that 'the powers that be' are to be obeyed in all matters concerned with the body, i.e., all political matters (while the Church concerned itself with spiritual affairs) ensured for Hitler the passivity (and sometimes even the approval) of the great majority of Protestants while he carried out his policies of rearmament, military expansion, the restriction of freedom and the liquidation of the Jews.

But Barth and his friends, notably Martin Niemöller, pastor in Berlin, Dietrich Bonhoeffer and Hanns Lilje, saw things differently. For them, the totalitarian claims of the State were a form of idolatry, and the teaching of the 'German Christians' (a group of Churchmen favourable to Hitler) that the recent history of Germany, with Hitler as saviour, was an act of God, ranked as sheer blasphemy. In 1934 they issued the Barmen Confession, an uncompromising assertion of the sovereignty of God over all human affairs and of the final revelation of God in Jesus Christ. They formed and organized the Confessing Church—the true Church, as they claimed, within the official Evangelical Churches. The Confessing Church gathered into its ranks a good number of the younger pastors, issued from underground a series of scathing criticisms of the regime on theological grounds, and set up a secret seminary for future pastors where lectures were given in the small hours of the morning. The disappearance of Niemöller into a concentration camp in 1937 was no surprise; and he was followed by several others.

THE DENOMINATIONS CARRY ON

Meanwhile on a less theological level the National Socialists had tried to turn the Protestant Churches into an instrument of state by forcing the many Churches of the various provinces into one Church under the control of a 'Reichsbischof', Ludwig Müller, who had been an army chaplain and had become Hitler's religious adviser. At this point bishops, pastors, congregations and theological faculties who had been at first quiescent rose in protest, for this was the interference of the State in *spiritual* matters. The protest was strongest in the south of the country, not least because Müller was a Prussian. In Tübingen, for instance, one of the greatest theological centres, the theological students held a mass meeting when they heard that Bishop Wurm of Württemberg had been put under house arrest for refusing to co-operate with Müller, made fiery speeches which made them liable to arrest, and rose to their feet to sing Luther's 'Ein' Feste Burg' (and Germans stand up to sing hymns only when they are moved to the depths of their being). Thus new recruits for the Confessing Churches were gained, and even those who did not join the Confessing Church were gravely disturbed.

The Scheme of compulsory unification proved unworkable, and Müller subsided into well-deserved obscurity.

It was against the background of these events that the second World Conference on Faith and Order was held in Edinburgh in 1937. It approved proposals for the setting up of a World Council of Churches, and appointed Commissions (which because of war could not report for fifteen years) on the Church, Ways of Worship and Inter-Communion, since these were the points where the chief differences between the Churches were focused.

'Life and Work' met again in Oxford in 1937, and added its approval to that of 'Faith and Order' to the formation of a World Council. Its proceedings were overshadowed by the emergence of dictatorships and the imminence of European war; and there was a deep division among the delegates between those who supported the pacifist approach to these problems and those who did not. Both approaches were argued theologically, but no real reconciliation achieved. But both in Edinburgh and Oxford in 1937 considerable unanimity was possible between the Churches and nations represented on other matters of social concern.

World conferences of this kind stimulate the spirit and the imagination of those who attend them to an immeasurable extent, but the necessary task of communicating the new insights gained to the non-attending ministers and people of the Churches involved had scarcely begun when the invasion of Poland put an abrupt end to official international conferences of every sort. Yet there was another ecumenical factor whose operation even war could not stop—in fact, it rather tended to further it. This was the enthusiasm of the young. Temple's Mission to Oxford in 1931 was made possible by the co-operation of all denominations in the University, and this fact is symbolical of the coming together of students to explore, profess and act upon one faith—in Oxford, Cambridge and other places, and especially perhaps in Cambridge, where the Free Churches were more strongly welcomed than elsewhere and the opportunity to come together more sought after and available. The rapprochement happened mostly under the aegis of the Student Christian Movement, which in the shape which it took at that time was the nursery of future ecumenical leaders; it is a matter of regret that the S.C.M., for the time being at least, does not seem now to fulfil that role.

Ecumenism, we know is for the sake of mission, and this was fully understood by Christian undergraduates in the thirties. Hence the interdenominational student campaigns, mostly to the industrial towns of Northern England. It was in preparation for these campaigns that many first suffered the pain—a pain not yet entirely healed—of not being able to take communion freely together with other Christians to whom they were bound by every chain of spiritual fellowship. The campaigns were large and spectacular occasions; there were also in the Universities smaller groups devoted to the cause of Christian unity. For instance, every year on Ascension Day ordinands from the denominational theological college in Cambridge met in Madingley Parish Church to pray for the reunion of Christ's Church.

In 1936 an actual Plan of Union for the Churches in

THE DENOMINATIONS CARRY ON

Britain, largely drawn up by the Baptist, Hugh Martin, and based on the application of the South India Scheme to Britain, emerged from the conversations that had gone on for so long. But there was no time to consider it properly before the outbreak of war in 1939, and when the War was over it was scarcely looked at again, though in fact it contains elements which have recurred in all subsequent discussions. Its very existence and the response that began to be made were enough to show that there were some at least in all the Churches who really meant business when they talked about Christian Unity, and would not be ultimately satisfied with talk—or even prayer—alone.

CHAPTER THREE

The Growth of the Ecumenical Idea

THE SECOND World War was not entered upon by the British in any flush of idealism, but one of grim and long-expected necessity. Evacuation from the large cities, conscription and rationing had been organized in advance, and the British nation was at least prepared psychologically, though militarily it was not. The romance of war had been killed in the trenches of the previous World War, and the possibility of the total obliteration of civilization was never absent from the mind. No one quite believed that Sir Robert Vansittart (in *Black Record*) was right in saying that there were no good Germans (for between the wars many British people had met many such), but detestation for the Hitler regime, its treatment of dissidents and defeated countries, and its attempted extermination of the Jews, was so profound that peace negotiations in 1940 (when a strong case could have been made out for them) were impossible, and the subsequent long-drawn-out hardships and losses remained endurable.

Perhaps it was this steadiness of purpose, with no violent oscillations between triumphant patriotism and bitter disillusionment, that created the most significant difference between the First and Second World Wars. Most of the men and women of the First World War simply wanted to return to the situation with which they were familiar and carry on as before. Those of the Second were planning for a new and better world even before victory was in sight. The civilian population was involved in the conduct of the war as never on any previous occasion—in industry, in Air Raid Precautions, in the Home Guard, in restrictions on food, clothing and travel (even to the extent of being deprived of signposts when traversing the countryside on its lawful occasions), in repairing the damage to house and home; and there was, as always

THE GROWTH OF THE ECUMENICAL IDEA

in wartime, a great weight of personal and private separation and sorrow also to bear. Yet, at least in the second half of the war, plans were being aired, and hopes were encouraged, of a more equal society, of better health and education for all, and of freedom from the perils of poverty, unemployment and old age. Certainly also the men and women in the Services, though this was not apparent until the result of the 1945 General Election was known, were not prepared to come back to a Britain where the old disparities between rich and poor, the priviledged and the deprived, were likely to be indefinitely maintained.

In this climate of thought, not unmixed, of course, with a strong dose of cynicism about the possibility, or even desirability, of real change in basic British attitudes, the Churches also looked to a better future for the world and for Britain. To some extent because each of them saw that the re-building of shattered premises and organizations, with reduced resources of people and finance, was going to be incredibly difficult (as, indeed, it was) for every denomination if it relied on itself, to some extent because it seemed absurd to many, in the circumstances of war and post-war, to put denominational differences above the Gospel held in common, and to some extent because pre-war ecumenical notions had taken root in the minds of many Christians now coming to leadership, active co-operation between Christians and between Churches began to occur in many geographical and social areas.

The Malvern Conference of 1941 on 'The Life of the Church and the Order of Society', inspired and led by William Temple, was almost entirely an Anglican affair, but it had repercussions far beyond the Church of England, especially when its spirit was expressed in Temple's *Christianity and Social Order* (1942), and it led to a great deal of interdenominational thinking. The British Council of Churches was founded in 1942, and later in the war there was a series of 'Religion and Life Weeks' in the cities and towns of Britain (the first was in Bristol, which had also seen the foundation of the first local Council of Churches, in 1925, as a direct result of the Copec Conference; the smallest place affected was Uppingham, in Rutland). In these weeks speakers of every denomination addressed multi-denominational audiences on the relation of the Christian Faith to personal, social, economic, political and international life.

When R. A. Butler was planning his Education Bill (enacted in 1944), the question of Religious Education naturally came to the fore, and the old squabbles about the Dual System and the subsidizing from the rates of Church Schools returned to people's minds—and often froze the hearts of administrators who remembered the past all too well. But this time a new spirit was abroad. The Free Churches were not greatly concerned to end the Dual System, though they retained reservations about Single School areas—for the Single School was nearly always Anglican. They directed their attention far more to the question of religious teaching in county schools, where, of course, the great majority of children received their education. And here they could make common cause with the Church of England.

'Religious Instruction' was, by common consent, a low grade subject in most schools, badly taught and indifferently received. In an effort to raise the standards expected and fulfilled, and to see that the teaching of the Bible formed a vital element in the building of post-war society, the Archbishops of Canterbury and York, the Roman Catholic Archbishop of Westminster, and the Moderator of the Free Church Council issued in 1944 a joint statement, the product of much spade-work behind the scenes by educational experts of all the Churches, calling for a proper emphasis on worship, the availability of good teaching on the Bible and the Faith for all children, and the improvement of facilities for the training of teachers in religious education.

The Education Act of 1944 embodied these requirements, insisting on a daily act of collective worship in every school and making it no longer necessary for the period of religious instruction to be the first of the day (so that it could be given throughout the school by those skilled in the subject). It further laid down that the teaching of religion (at that time assumed to be the Christian religion) should be according to an 'Agreed Syllabus'. The experiment of calling together teachers, clergy and ministers of various denominations, and

THE GROWTH OF THE ECUMENICAL IDEA

members of the local authority, to compose a syllabus for religious teaching had been tried out successfully in Cambridgeshire, and each local authority was now required to set up a conference with the same constituent members for the same purpose. The local authorities obeyed, and the result was a multiplicity of Agreed Syllabuses, some very much in line with modern scholarships, others not so much, but all designed to influence the pupils in the direction of Christianity, and, typically of the age, to improve their social behaviour and personal ethics.

Some Anglicans objected that Agreed Syllabuses were bound to contain a diluted Christian faith, since members of Churches suspected of being not so orthodox as themselves had a hand in them. But these objections turned out to be without foundation, and, indeed, the co-operation between the Churches required for the creation of Agreed Syllabuses was one of the factors that revealed to startled Anglicans and Free Churchmen how much of Christian doctrine they had in common with each other. The defects of the Syllabuses were rather that they were over-academic, produced for the most part by Biblical scholars who were not kept sufficiently aware of the spiritual and intellectual capacities of ordinary people by their school-teacher colleagues; and that (although this was not realized until many years later) they were too authoritarian in approach, not sufficiently open to the inquiring, critical, and often sceptical mind of youth. More recent Agreed Syllabuses prescribed a great deal less in the way of formal teaching, and suggest a great deal more in the way of open, uncommitted discussion of major ethical and religious questions.

William Temple, at his enthronement as Archbishop of Canterbury in 1942 declared that 'the ecumenical movement is the great new fact of our era'. It is doubtful whether all those who have regularly quoted (or misquoted) this sentence from that day to this have a clear idea of what he really meant by 'the ecumenical movement'. It is the expression of an idea which was only then beginning to take definite shape even in Temple's mind, and his death two years later halted for a time the process by which it was being steadily formulated

41

in the minds of the groups of people all over Christendom.

It is therefore perhaps useful at this point to try and see through to the heart of this idea. In essence it is an idea—springing from biblical, catholic theology, expressed in worship, and issuing in a vision and a way of life—about the Lordship of Christ in his Church. According to it, the Church of which Christ is Lord, is one, and one only; there can be no duality or plurality at this point, any more than there can be two or more Gods, or two or more Christs. This oneness is the gift of God, Father, Son and Holy Spirit, and cannot by any human sin or blunder be destroyed, though men and women, including Christians and Christian communities, may misunderstand it or refuse to receive it. The Church is one, in both senses of the word 'one': there is no Church but the Church; and it cannot be divided into portions or sections, any more than Christ can be divided.

The Church does not exist for itself alone, nor is its unity an end in itself. To the one Church are committed the Gospel to study, explore, expound and preach to the whole world; the worship of God in Trinity which is the appropriate tribute of the creation, in heaven and on earth, to the Creator and Saviour and Guide; the service of all mankind in the manner of Jesus the Servant; and the hope of the Kingdom of God, which came in Jesus, which continually comes, and which is yet to come in its fullness. The Holy Spirit makes possible the fulfilment of this manifold commission by the gifts and power which he bestows on the whole people of God and on the men and women of which it is composed.

In the course of history this one Church has been broken up into many churches. But the essential unity which is God's gift has not been broken. The manifestation of that unity in human affairs, in worship and prayer, in theology and the ordering of the Christian life, social, ecclesiastical and personal, has been made temporarily impossible by separations among Christians and the refusal to heal these separations once they have been made.

The unity of the Church is not monolithic, though this truth was not at first clearly seen; within it there are varieties of theological thought, of liturgical modes and practice, of

THE GROWTH OF THE ECUMENICAL IDEA

devotional methods, of ethical approaches, of national and cultural styles of life and feeling and thinking. But these varieties are all contained within the one Church. Separations of those who wish to worship in one way from those who wish to worship in another way are the transformation of legitimate differences within one whole into distinct and independent entities which have no right to exist as such, but claim existence nonetheless.

The variegated unity of the Church is embodied in the one baptism, the one faith, the one ministry and the one eucharist; and in the celebration of the one eucharist all the varieties are taken up and presented to God as the one act of worship of the one Church.

It follows from all this that a Christian can have no greater concern than to heal the outward divisions of the Church, however long the task may take; and that his membership of the one Church takes precedence over his membership of any individual denomination. But it does not follow that he is to repudiate or neglect his membership of his denomination; on the contrary he is to live a faithful member of his denomination, in order that it may use the more fully the gifts which in spite of its separation it receives from the Spirit, share them with other denominations and treasure them against the day when it can contribute them to the whole Church manifested again as one.

This is the 'ecumenical idea', and to use the word 'ecumenical' in any sense which is less than the one here suggested is, in a way, to degrade it. We can, and do, use it of useful and pleasant things like joint services, united trips to the Holy Land and acts of co-operation in visiting the houses of a neighbourhood while collecting for Christian Aid, but they are ecumenical in the real sense only if the motive is the unity of Christ's Church and the purpose is the manifestation of that unity. Of course the 'lesser' acts of ecumenicity, if these conditions are fulfilled, serve many good purposes and establish the beginnings of a deeper understanding and a fuller fellowship, but they must not be mistaken for the real thing, or used as an excuse for not going forward to the goal which is set before us, however distant that goal may seem to be.

THE CHURCH IN OUR TIMES

This is the essence of the ecumenical idea; embryonic at first even in the minds of its greatest proponents, it has proved itself capable of development in many directions, but the core of the matter remains what it has been from the beginning.

It was the germination and maturing of the ecumenical idea that created, by a steady process, the World Council of Churches—not a world Church, be it noted, but a *Council* of Churches. We have seen that the leaders of 'Faith and Order' and 'Life and Work' had agreed in 1937 that such a Council was desirable, not least for the purpose of co-ordinating and reinforcing the two movements. A 'Provisional Committee' soon came into existence, representing the great majority of the non-Roman and non-Orthodox Churches of the world, charged with the task of bringing the Council into existence and calling its first Assembly; the Roman Catholic and Orthodox Churches were fully informed about its actions and proposals, and 'observed' them from a respectable distance. It might have been thought that the outbreak of the Second World War would impose a complete stoppage on the work of the Committee. But Geneva, which had already become the unofficial centre of ecumenical activity, was in a neutral country, and could be visited by members of the warring nations as well as by those from other neutral countries. There were obstacles in the way of such visits, of course, but they never entirely ceased, although no one could reach Geneva from England after the total occupation of France in 1942. And when personal visits were impossible, correspondence could be arranged. As a result, and with increasing momentum, the Provisional Committee drew up its plans—and, if necessary, scrapped them when the prolongation of the war put them out of court, and then made some more.

In October 1945—the Japanese war was just over—a delegation of American, British, Dutch, French and Swiss churchmen met the new Council of the Evangelical Church of Germany (now voluntarily united on a federal basis) in Stuttgart. Clearly it was essential to gain the co-operation of the German Church if the World Council of Churches was to be in any sense worthy of its name; and, equally clearly, it was

THE GROWTH OF THE ECUMENICAL IDEA

doubtful whether the Germans were in a position to agree to such co-operation. But fears were ungrounded; the German Church leaders responded to the invitation by signing the 'Stuttgart Declaration' in which they acknowledged their share in the guilt of the German people and expressed a strong desire to re-enter the ecumenical fellowship. One of the leading personalities in the framing of the declaration was Pastor Niemöller, who had spent much of the war in a concentration camp and was certainly damaged in health; but he was also filled with an unconquerable zeal for the renewal of the German Church and of its links with the rest of Christendom.

There was need also to discover the attitude of the Orthodox Churches of Russia and the Middle East. The Orthodox Church of Russia turned down the invitation to share in the formation of the Council, being under the impression—derived, no doubt, from a misunderstanding of the ecumenical idea—that the World Council would set itself up as an 'ecumenical church' and become a centre of political power. But other Orthodox Churches—including those of Constantinople and Greece—were dissuaded from following the Russian example, and co-operated in the meeting of the first Assembly.

This met for worship in Amsterdam on August 22nd 1948, composed of 351 delegates from 147 churches in 44 countries, and on the following day the World Council of Churches came into existence. The theme of its deliberations was 'Man's Disorder and God's Design', and different sections studied the theme in its aspects of Church unity, missionary and evangelistic activity, and the need for bringing order into national and international economics and politics.

The Assembly caught the imagination of Christians all over the world who were looking for a Christian lead through the complexities and dangers of the post-war period, as well as of all who prayed for Christian unity. The Message of the Assembly to the world, largely drawn up, it is widely believed, in the words of Daniel T. Niles, the young Methodist leader from Ceylon, caught the imagination even more: 'Christ has made us his own, and He is not divided. In seeking Him we find one another. Here at Amsterdam we have committed ourselves afresh to Him, and have covenanted with one another in constituting the World Council of Churches. We intend to stay together.'

The first General Secretary of the W.C.C. was Visser t'Hooft, of the Netherlands, and his powerful mind held the Council together at all times of stress in the years that followed.

Second only to William Temple as a British leader in ecumenical affairs, and now his natural successor, was Bishop G. K. A. Bell of Chichester. Bell had been heavily engaged in the Life and Work Movement since the Stockholm Conference of 1925, and eager to see the foundation of the World Council. During the war he maintained contact with German Church leaders, such as Dietrich Bonhoeffer and Hanns Lilje, and was the friend of some of those who took part in the July 30th 1944 plot to assassinate Hitler (though no one supposes him to have been implicated). In the closing years of the war he protested publicly against the saturation bombing of German cities, and may have forfeited thereby his chance of succeeding William Temple as Archbishop of Canterbury.

A few months before the Amsterdam Assembly, there came into existence the first Church formed from a union of episcopal and non-episcopal Churches, the Church of South India. The date was September 1947, and the year was the year of India's independence. Negotiations had been proceeding for 28 years, and the final draft of the Scheme that was adopted was published in 1942. It had, of course, to gain, if possible, the approval not only of the South India Christian people, but also of the British Churches from which the uniting Churches were derived. The necessary approval was gained, though certain restrictions on full communication were imposed by the Church of England.

The inaugural service was held in St George's Cathedral, Madras, and the preacher was the Methodist J. S. M. Hooper, known as 'the pilot of South India Union'. He said: 'God has matched us with this hour; the Church of South India has an unparalleled opportunity. The reconciliation between our divergent elements—enables us with fresh conviction and force to proclaim the Gospel of reconciliation to all the clashing elements in this nation's life. The eucharistic service of inauguration was most carefully drawn up to include elements from Greek, Anglican, Methodist and Swedish sources. The C.S.I. was formed of Anglicans, Methodists and the United Church of South India. The Church was episcopal. The ordaining ministries of all the uniting Churches were mutually accepted from the start, and the bishops of the various dioceses were appointed from their number, some being Anglican, some Presbyterian, some Congregationalist and some Methodist. All ordinations subsequent to the inauguration were episcopal. Congregations which could not in conscience accept the ministrations of 'presbyters' (as clergy and ministers were now called) who had been ordained in a way alien to their traditions were exempted from having to do so. It is was agreed that thirty years later, in 1977, the Church would deliberate whether any exceptions to episcopal ordination were still to be allowed (the date set has now been passed, and the deliberation has proved unnecessary).

Ever since its inauguration the C.S.I. has been an example and an incentive throughout the Christian world. No doubt it has gone through periods of tension and misunderstanding, but there has never been any move to unmake the union. On the contrary, the Church has gone forward on the path which it has chosen (or was chosen for it by the Holy Spirit, as its members would say), creating and building its own traditions of liturgy, devotion, evangelism and service, but never losing contact with its sister Churches in the ecumenical fellowship. If others have been slow to follow its example, pointing out, by way of excuse, faults in its make-up, it has silently replied by its steady continuance that others need not follow it in detail but are surely called to emulate its spirit.

CHAPTER FOUR

Advances and Rebuffs 1945-60

THE CASUALTY lists of many countries were shorter in the Second World War than in the First; but in all other respects the Second was immensely more destructive. The first and extended task of each belligerent nation was to reconstruct not only its buildings but the whole fabric of its economic and political life—except only for the U.S.A., which had suffered least, but was now called upon to provide a large proportion of the resources needed to re-build the rest of the world.

The task of reconstruction was greatest in Germany, where most of the large cities had to be re-built almost from the ground. In the Federal Republic American aid and the incredible industriousness and determination of the people combined to complete the major part of the work as quickly as it was done where the damage was much less; in the Democratic Republic nothing much was allowed to happen by the Soviets for some years to come. Britain decided to combine its building programme with the nationalization of the Bank of England and some key industries, the institution of the Welfare State, the re-designing of the educational system and the dismantling of the Empire; and at the same time had to face the menace from the East with military forces which were difficult to maintain in any strength (and would of course have been useless without the American alliance).

As it was with nations, so also was it with the Churches within the nations, except again for America. Continental church structures, both literal and metaphorical, were in ruins. The leadership was decimated, and great numbers of men were still prisoners of war in Russia. In Britain it was mostly, but not only, the actual buildings that had been destroyed, though on nothing like the German scale, and the grim necessity of repairing war damage could be expected to

ADVANCES AND REBUFFS 1945-60

preoccupy the Church authorities, and at the same time to turn their minds to co-operation in fields where resources could be economized by this means. Both these things happened, but not to the full extent. Characteristic of the British, perhaps, is a readiness to forgive and forget past enmities; certainly the British Churches were willing to contribute generously, out of much reduced and much needed resources, to the funds of the World Council of Churches' Inter Church Aid (later re-named Christian Aid) for the re-building of churches and seminaries, and the financial assistance of theological students, as well as for the care of the numberless 'displaced persons' and refugees of every sort over the whole face of Europe. At the same time, alliances of respect and affection were formed between cities and churches on opposite sides of the North Sea and the Channel; Bristol, for instance, already by tradition an ecumenical city, was able to form and sustain alliances with Bordeaux (though not in this case on an ecclesiastical level) and Hanover. The bishop of Lower Saxony, Hanns Lilje, was an ecumenical friend from student days and the World Student Federation of Bishop Cockin of Bristol, and this personal link ensured that church links at many levels, parochial and civic, were established.

In Britain at least, it was no longer acceptable to most Churches to organize activities on a purely denominational basis; a certain infusion, not too strong, of ecumenical spirit was widely thought to be desirable. The Methodist Church initiated a series of 'Commando Campaigns', which were not entirely unsuccessful efforts to bring the preaching of the Gospel in intelligible terms to the shop floor and the class room; and having done this, it invited ministers and laymen of other Churches to join in—which some did. But it is not truly ecumenical for one Church to plan and launch a project, and *then* invite the help of others; the habit of doing this is ingrained both in Methodists and Anglicans. And alongside the increase of inter-Church co-operation there was an upsurge generally, and not least in Britain, of denominationalism.

At the level of the local parish and congregation ecumenical activity was slow in growing, though widely accepted as good in principle. In many places, at least before the advent of television on the large scale, Christians went to 'their own church' on Sundays and weekdays to satisfy social and cultural needs as well as to worship God, and many Churches were still, therefore, the foci of self-sufficient communities to which ecumenism made little appeal. In several areas of some large cities—Manchester, Birmingham and Bristol particularly—inter-Church co-operation in study and worship and witness did grow steadily, but it tended on the whole to involve only those few who were especially interested, the ecumenical élite, as they might, ironically or seriously, be called.

British Universities, increased and increasing in numbers and size, now included far more men and women from the classes in society where Free Churchmen were most numerous. The John Wesley Society in Oxford, for example, went from a pre-war figure of less than fifty to more than two hundred. This was not due simply to an increase in the size of the constituency. It expressed a new, almost exclusive emphasis on denominational identity (not by any means a bad thing in the case of freshmen and freshwomen, who often arrived at Universities in profound ignorance of what the Church believed and stood for, but scarcely necessary as the students became more mature), which edged the Student Christian Movement away from the centre of University religious life, and ultimately limited it to the social concerns of the radical minority. This happened more gradually in other Universities than in Oxford where the S.C.M. retained its strength into the late fifties. But an absurd situation arose in many Universities by which a new 'Christian Association' had to be formed to bring together the religious societies, with the Student Christian Movement as just one not very important member. The more evangelical students remained faithful to the various Christian Unions, which were unabated in size and influence. The S.C.M., in fact, was more effective in the Sixth Forms of Schools, for which it set up a separate organization, than in Universities.

Even more threatening (as some thought) to the Ecumenical Movement was the growth of World Confessional organizations. This arose in the first place quite naturally out of the desire of American Christians to help their co-denominationalists in other less fortunate parts of the world. Largely because of American generosity, Baptists, Congregationalists, Lutherans, Presbyterians, Methodists and others foregathered to discuss and further their common traditions. Then the Baptist World Alliance, the Lutheran World Federation and the World Methodist Council (to name only the largest) acquired a global organization with regular world conferences. So far, so good, for each Christian tradition needs to be renewed from time to time, and there is no better way of doing this than by the interchange of ideas and the sharing of worship between those who hold the traditions in different forms. But the growing strength of these organizations fostered the concept in some minds of a World Lutheran *Church*, or a World Methodist *Church*, or a World Reformed *Church*, in a world that was crying out, not for the accentuation but for the reconciliation of denominational differences.

The theological climate, however, was not favourable to denominationalism. In the first place, the company of international scholars who applied new scientific procedures to Biblical, doctrinal and church-historical studies, and who made use of—and sometimes contradicted—each other's findings, had little use of denominational labels, and were content to place their services at the disposal of the whole Christian public, and of the Faith and Order Movement of the World Council of Churches when invited to do so. In Britain, Old Testament research tended to be in the hands of Baptists, the New Testament in the hands of Methodists and Congregationalists, Church History in the hands of Anglicans, and systematic theology in the hands of Anglicans and Presbyterians, but there were many exceptions to this, and the unprecedented sight began to be seen of Free Church theological books on the shelves of Anglican clergymen, and vice versa.

In the second place, one of the major assured findings of the new schools of Biblical scholars was that the concept of the Church, with a whole host of Old Testament antecedents, occupies a central place in New Testament living and thinking. The New Testament Church, it now became apparent, was deeply felt by its members to be both the People of God and the organically unified Body of Christ. John Robinson, later to be famous in another connexion, seemed to maintain in *The Body* that the word 'Body' was used here quite literally in the New Testament. But even if, as seems most likely, 'People' and 'Body' were both used in metaphorical senses, the metaphors arose from a profound consciousness of togetherness in Christ, and of the will of Christ himself to be one with his 'members'. This Church was not greatly institutionalized in the New Testament; in fact the new studies lent force to the contention of B. H. Streeter in *The Primitive Church* (1929), fiercely controverted at the time of its writing, that there were the seeds of episcopacy, presbyterianism *and* congregationalism in New Testament thinking. But it was not formless and purely spiritual; it was in fact an 'organized' Church in embryo. Much of this had been disclosed in the pre-war book of the Methodist, R. Newton Flew, *Jesus and his Church*, and had administered shocks all round. But the shocks had now been absorbed, and the discovery became a basic part of New Testament scholarship.

In the third place, although the early theology of Karl Barth was not accepted in full for long even by his closest followers, and was indeed modified by Barth himself in his later years, it had the positive effect of placing the Bible again squarely in the centre of Christian theology, in a place above that of the Church. From this came the impetus for the formulation of 'Biblical Theology', which accepted the results of Biblical criticism, but placed the dominant themes of both Testaments ('covenant', 'exodus', 'salvation', the Messianic hope and its realization, the 'Kingdom of God', the 'People of God', and the 'coming of the Lord' in glory) in the context of a coherent proclamation ('kerygma') by the early Church of 'the mighty acts of God'. It was denied that what we have in the Bible is ever just bare historical narrative; it is always history with a meaning, and the meaning is the activity of God for the salvation of mankind. Even the mysterious sayings of Jesus about his return to earth and the coming of the Kingdom of God could be fitted into this scheme, since, according to C. H.

ADVANCES AND REBUFFS 1945–60

Dodd, the eschatology (i.e. account of the 'last things', usually thought to be reserved for the end of time) of the Bible was 'realized' (i.e. made real and contemporary) by the coming of Jesus and his ministry of words and deeds.

Clearly this was a theology which was irrespective of denominations; and those who preached it and those who heard it with understanding were not likely to make heavy weather of denominational arguments about the ministry and the sacraments.

But there were articulate groups of people, especially in the Anglo-Catholic section of the Church of England, who stood aside from the movements in theology which have just been described, partly consciously, because such theology was dangerous to Catholic truth as they saw it, partly for the simple, unconscious reason that their understanding of Christianity and the traditions of their Church life had no place for it. Giving a very high place to the sacramental life and nourishing their souls with frequent participation in the Eucharist, disposed to regard the phrase 'Body of Christ' as an almost literal description of the Church, and seeing in the historical episcopate, validated by Apostolic Succession, the divinely appointed keystone of Church Order, they could not but regard an ecumenism which seemed to them to ask for the immediate destruction of denominational barriers with grave disfavour; and the foundation of the Church of South India, with its recognition of non-episcopal ministers, was an affront to their deepest principles.

The most powerful group of these was gathered round the immensely learned Kenneth Kirk, Bishop of Oxford, and the equally learned Gregory Dix, monk of Nashdom Abbey. In *The Apostolic Ministry* (1946), Kirk, the editor, states unequivocally that the view of all the writers is that 'the episcopate is the divinely appointed ministerial instrument for securing to the Church of God its continuous and organic unity, not as a club of like-minded worshippers or aspirants to holiness, but as a God-given city of salvation'. From this he goes on to distinguish the 'essential' ministry, which is that of the bishop, given to him by Christ through the succession of bishops from the apostles; and the 'dependent' ministry,

53

which is that of the priests and deacons, derived from and subordinate to that of the bishops.

In the longest and most powerful chapter in the book, Dix argues that the Greek word 'apostolos' ('apostle', literally, 'one sent forth') is a translation of the Aramaic word (and Jesus spoke Aramaic) 'shaliach' (also meaning 'one sent forth'); he contends that in Jewish usage a 'shaliach' is a plenipotentiary, possessing all the powers by delegation which belong to the one who 'sends him out'; and he concludes that each apostle or 'shaliach' of Jesus had the full powers that Jesus had. And since one of the powers that a shaliach, or plenipotentiary, has is that of appointing a successor with the same powers as he has himself, those appointed by the apostles, i.e. the bishops, were plenipotentiaries of Jesus and able to appoint their successors, again with the same powers.

Dix's theory was strongly contested when it appeared, and most effectively by T. W. Manson, the Congregationalist, on the ground of its having quite inadequate support in the actual role of a Jewish 'shaliach' (who often had only temporary powers) and in the words and actions of Jesus himself. No one, probably, now holds the theory as Dix expounded it, but it had considerable effect in moulding Anglo-Catholic thought on the episcopal office.

Another, but brief, collection of Anglo-Catholic essays was *Catholicity* (1947), which supported the general position of *The Apostolic Ministry*. The essayists included T. S. Eliot, and denied that protestants held the full Christian faith or the true Christian ministry. The reply of *The Catholicity of Protestantism* (edited by R. Newton Flew and the present writer) (1950) claimed the fullness of Biblical faith for protestants, and set out the Scriptural grounds for the protestant doctrine of the ministry. The tone of both these works was sharper than most people would now think necessary or desirable, but it reflected the contemporary temper on both sides of this particular argument.

Catholicity and *The Catholicity of Protestantism*, together with a third work, *The Fullness of Christ*, by a group of Anglican Evangelicals, had all been called for by Geoffrey

ADVANCES AND REBUFFS 1945-60

Fisher, Archbishop of Canterbury in succession to William Temple, as a follow up to his epoch-making (the word is correctly used) 'Cambridge Sermon' of November, 1946. The credit for the 'breakthrough' that this sermon made possible will be given to Archbishop Fisher long after his less helpful later entrances on the ecumenical scene are mercifully forgotten.

The text of the Sermon was John 10:9–10: 'I am the Door; by me if any man enter in, he shall be saved and shall go in and out, and find pasture. The thief cometh not but for to steal and to kill and to destroy: I am come that they might have life and that they might have it more abundantly' (AV). It is hard to see the logical connexion between this text and the main burden of what followed (as is not unusual in sermons). But the reference to the abundant life which the Saviour came to give led the Archbishop to point out at the beginning that the divine life which flows from Christ does not freely circulate between the various 'folds', or denominations, 'in the life-giving operations of worship to Him who is the Head of the Church and of sacramental fellowship between His members'. 'The circulation of the Church's lifeblood is impaired or blocked: and thereby of necessity its work and witness in a world distraught and for men without a spiritual anchorage, is grievously enfeebled.' And all this, the Archbishop claimed, was because the different 'folds' were 'fenced off from one another by barriers, some trivial enough, some reaching up (as it would seem) to heaven itself, which the long course of the Church's history has erected.

To heal this dreadful disease, the sermon went on, various schemes of constitutional reunion had been suggested. But these did not offer at this time the right way to union in England, for three reasons: (i) The Church of England is an established Church, with a very complicated legal nexus with the State. To accept the establishment as it stands was impossible for Free Churchmen; to amend it in a way which would satisfy all parties would take decades. (ii) The Church of England is the 'nodal point' of the Anglican worldwide communion. For it to leave this communion would disrupt the communion itself. (iii) The Church of England is in the

55

process of resolving its own inner tensions and recovering its spiritual authority; it could not wisely be involved for the present in 'questions of constitutional affiliations to other denominations'.

Dr Fisher therefore suggested another 'way forward'. This was that 'while the folds remain distinct, there should be a movement towards a free and unfettered exchange of life in worship and sacrament between them as there is already of prayer and thought and Christian fellowship—in short, that they should grow towards that full communion with one another, which already in their separation they have with Christ'. And the means which he proposed by which that 'growth into full communion' could be initiated and expedited was that the Free Churches should take 'episcopacy into their systems'; he himself, as an Anglican bishop, would thankfully receive at the hands of others 'their commission in their accustomed form', and similarly confer an Anglican commission on them.

He did not wish, he said, the Free Churches to accept Anglican episcopacy as it was; for 'the Church of England has not yet found the finally satisfying use of episcopacy in practice'. They had already agreed to the acceptance of episcopacy in all the schemes of reunion that had been propounded; here was their opportunity to 'try out' episcopacy 'on their own ground'—and find the kind of episcopacy that suited their spiritual requirements. Thus, without sacrificing any principles or being induced to make constitutional arrangements with which they were not entirely happy, they would come to possess a ministry 'mutually acknowledged by all as possessing not only the inward call of the Spirit but also the authority which each Church in conscience requires'—in accordance with the Lambeth Appeal of 1920.

Without doubt, the proposal that the Free Churches should 'take episcopacy into their systems' was new, exciting and hopeful. The Free Churches readily agreed to send representatives to a Joint Conference with representatives of the Church of England, convened to work out carefully and in detail the implications of the Cambridge Sermon. This Joint Conference, having met frequently for three years, produced in 1950 a booklet called *Church Relations in England*. This was deliberately *not* an attempt to outline a scheme for intercommunion or union; it was a working out of what action would have to be taken if any Free Church or Churches wished to adopt Dr Fisher's proposal; it did not urge any Free Church to do this, but merely stated what would be involved by its doing so.

The Joint Conference laid it down that any negotiations for the establishment of intercommunion would have to be conducted in a parallel series between the Church of England on the one hand and individual Free Churches on the other, not in a single operation between the Church of England and all the Free Churches together. It further indicated that for such negotiations to have any chance of success the following conditions would have to be fulfilled: (a) the negotiating Churches would have to be satisfied with each other's loyalty to the apostolic faith; (b) the Free Churches would 'take episcopacy into their systems' by accepting an episcopate consecrated through bishops in the historic succession, and by adopting episcopal ordination in the future; (c) the Church of England would agree to admit to Holy Communion baptized communicant members of the Free Churches and authorize its own members to receive Communion from such Free Church ministers as had been consecrated to the episcopate, episcopally ordained, or 'further commissioned' to the presbyterate; (d) the Free Churches would think seriously of adopting episcopal confirmation; (e) any Free Church which became episcopal would maintain the relations of fellowship and intercommunion which it already enjoyed with non-episcopal Churches; (f) it would be recognized by the Churches involved in negotiation that the continued existence of two Churches in the same area was only a temporary stage on the road to full unity. These were the conditions, and in the course of comments on them the Joint Conference pointed out that it was assumed that the same liberty of interpretation of the nature of episcopacy and priesthood would be accorded by the negotiating parties to each other as already obtained in the Church of England.

After a decent period for the digestion of these far-reaching implications of the Cambridge Sermon, the Church of England and the Methodist Church corresponded with each other about the conditions indicated by the Joint Conference. The Methodist Church obtained assurances that any discussions with the Church of England would be regarded as taking place *within* the Body of Christ (and not between people who had broken away from the Body of Christ and the Body of Christ itself). The Church of England obtained a Methodist assurance that the office and functions of a priest in the Church of God would be safeguarded in the ordinal and practice of the Methodist Church if it took episcopacy into its system.

On the basis of the conditions stated in *Church Relations in England*, and the correspondence between the Church of England and the Methodist Church, these two Churches in 1955 instituted official 'Conversations' with a view to the establishment of intercommunion between them. The original leader of the Anglican team of twelve was Dr Bell, Bishop of Chichester, but he died during the course of the Conversations, and his place was taken in 1958 by Dr Carpenter, Bishop of Oxford. The leader of the twelve Methodists was Dr Harold Roberts, Principal of Richmond College, Surrey.

It is sometimes said that the Conversations would have had a greater chance of being ultimately successful if they had included other Free Churches, but even if the notion that bilateral conversations offered the best way forward had been abandoned, the fact remains that only the Methodist Church among the Free Churches was ready at that time to take part in official conversations.

Other conversations in the British Isles had been taking place for a long period of years before Dr Fisher preached his notable sermon, and these were between the Church of England and the Church of Scotland; the Scottish Episcopal Church and the Presbyterian Church of England had joined in later. The conversations had languished somewhat since the thirties, but were stirred into new life by the Cambridge Sermon. In 1953 a report from the negotiators that announced 'full unity' as the goal was accepted by the

ADVANCES AND REBUFFS 1945-60

Churches concerned. But when a definite proposal was made in 1957 that presbyterianism and episcopacy should be combined by the appointment of 'bishops in presbytery' (that is, the bishops would work, not independently, but in and with the presbytery, which contained both ministers and lay elders), a storm of largely (but, of course, not wholly) irrational opposition burst over the heads of the unhappy negotiators. Lord Beaverbrook, owner of the *Scottish Daily Express*, for reasons of his own which were not fully apparent to others (he had some Presbyterian antecedents in his home country of Canada), whipped up nationalistic fury in the pages of his paper, and supposedly responsible leaders even suggested that the whole thing was a secret ecclesiastical plot to enslave the Scots to the English. Despite the absurdity of many of the arguments employed to oppose the Scheme, the General Assembly of the Church of Scotland resolved in 1959 that the Bishops' Report implied 'a denial of the catholicity of the Church of Scotland and of the validity and regularity of its ministry within the Church Catholic'. It is clear that some sore points in the Scottish religious consciousness had been inadvertently touched. The Church of England did not discuss the Report, as it was already defunct; no one can do more than guess what its response would have been.

An attempt was subsequently made to revive the issue by appointing a large commission of 150, with representatives from all four participating Churches. This covered useful ground in the early sixties, ultimately recommending conversations in each country designed to bring about a united Church in England and a united Church in Scotland in communion with each other. But the final result was a slow grinding to a halt.

It was easy, as the fifties ended, to be entirely despondent about the prospects for reunion in Britain. But Archbishop Fisher's initiative was still operating.

59

CHAPTER FIVE

The World is the Scene

THE CHURCHES in Britain are quite a small part of the world Church, yet it is hard to discern traces of influences from outside Britain in the British ecumenical debates of the fifties and sixties. Even the inauguration of the Church of South India, which was an inspiration to many Christians all over the world, was more a matter of theological debate than an example to many British Christians.

There is some excuse for this insularity. Britain has its own distinctive history of constant rivalry and sometimes bitter conflict between different traditions, and its own tortuous development of relationships between Church and State. Ecumenical activity is therefore particularly complex and arduous, and has to be carried out, if it is to be effective, in the ways demanded by the British situation. The formation and constitution of the Church of South India could scarcely form a model, without more ado, for Church unity in Britain.

British theologians and Church leaders, after the time of William Temple, were, nevertheless, unduly imprevious, even resistant, to ecumenical ideas from abroad, and overseas observers certainly detected a good deal of parochialism in their ways of proceeding. Some new ways of thinking and some entirely new concepts—such as, in the fifties, the notion that the Church, like individual Christians, is both 'justified' and 'sinful'—did, however, filter through from the tumult of discussion that characterizes world ecumenical conferences, and were in due course fed into the British discussions, though their origins were not always acknowledged.

At the same time, from taking the leading part at ecumenical conferences, it came to be the role of British participants not to make great prophetic utterances or open up entirely new fields of thought, but to select, tidy up, formulate, organize and transcribe the most promising ideas from the minds of Germans, Americans, and, increasingly towards the end of this period, thinkers from the Third World.

The Third World Conference on Faith and Order was held in Lund, in South Sweden, in 1952. The Oecumenical Patriarch of Constantinople sent a message to the Conference to say that those representing the Orthodox Churches under his jurisdiction were not present to *discuss* any aspects of the Christian Faith, but only to *expound* the Faith as it is unerringly received in the Orthodox Churches. After the reading out of this message, the Orthodox delegates participated quite freely in the Conference, but they did not vote on its final Report. There was a slight difficulty in the matter of precedence in the procession to the official Conference services. It is the ecumenical practice for alphabetical order to determine the processional order. The Orthodox representatives were not happy with this arrangement, and asked to be allotted the position at the head of the procession, which was for them the place of highest honour. This was granted to them, and no one was worried, since for most Churches the position at the rear is the most honourable.

Roman Catholic theologians were present in small numbers as 'press correspondents', and took no active part in the discussions. So unwilling was the Roman Catholic Church to be involved in the proceedings that the section in the preliminary report on 'the Church' which gave the Roman Catholic position had to be written—as a remarkable *tour de force*—by Newton Flew, the British Methodist.

The Lund Conference marked a decisive change of direction in the Faith and Order movement. Reports, commissioned at Edinburgh in 1937 and subsequently, but badly delayed by the war, on the Church, Intercommunion and Ways of Worship, were duly presented—and, to the chagrin of many of those who had produced them, scarcely discussed. One reason for this was that the copies of the chief of these reports, that on the Church, intended for the American participants, reached the United States after the participants had left for Europe (the ships carrying the reports and the theologians must have passed each other in mid-Atlantic);

but the deeper reason was the strong conviction of the Conference that the days of 'comparative ecclesiology' were over and a new period had begun. The reports had mostly comprised a series of statements by the Churches of their official positions on the subjects in question. Now it was generally agreed, at the instance of T. F. Torrance of the Church of Scotland, that Christians had to get behind and below their denominational differences to a common confession of the Lordship of Christ and the power of the Holy Spirit, and to build their common witness on this foundation. The mandate was given to the Commission which continued the work of the Conference to conduct a world-wide study on these lines. The mandate was, in the upshot, not fully carried out, since other more urgent concerns intervened, though the first steps were taken, and useful material collected. But the fact that the mandate was given at all indicates that a fresh start was being made.

Edinburgh 1937 had begun the consideration of 'non-theological factors' in the making and un-making of Church Union, and had commissioned a further study. This was taken up at Lund in quite a big way, and served as a most important corrective to the academic notion, sometimes unchallenged in ecumenical discussions, that relations between Churches are governed entirely by doctrinal considerations. The discussions at Lund showed that social factors of every kind, notably class and race differences and political developments, were at least as influential as any theology of the Church and the Ministry, and subsequent events connected with every effort to bring Churches together have borne this out in overwhelming measure.

The progress made at Lund towards Christian unity is indicated by a question which appears in the Conference's *Word to the Churches*: 'Should not our Churches ask themselves . . . whether they should not act together in all matters, except those in which deep differences of conviction compel them to act separately?' The positive notion which this question implies came to be called 'the Lund principle' (first propounded in Lund by Oliver Tomkins, then Secretary of the Faith and Order Department in Geneva, later Bishop of

THE WORLD IS THE SCENE

Bristol). It has often been misinterpreted to mean that Churches should act together in all matters in which it is inconvenient to act separately—or even that so long as they act together it does not greatly matter whether what they do is worth doing at all. But if it had been implemented in its proper sense by all, or even some, of the Churches represented at Lund, the present situation would be very different from what it actually is.

One of the most impressive addresses, though it did not greatly influence the final findings, was given by Edmund Schlink, of Heidelberg, on the Church as the 'Pilgrim People' of God. The pilgrimage of the Church, he said, was through very barren, even hostile land, but its goal was the city of God; and the time of the pilgrimage lasted from the first coming of Christ to the second. The Church was to be concerned, almost solely, with the salvation and protection of its members and itself, by faith and hope, from the indifferent and hostile forces which encompassed it; the secular world was so far gone in evil that it was irredeemable. This vision of the situation and role of the Church was clearly influenced by the grim experience through which the German Confessing Church had come, but it revealed a great difference in thinking from that of the theologians from Britain and the United States, who still believed that human society in all its parts be brought under the rule of God.

Equally shocking to the Americans was the statement made to the press during the Conference by Joseph Hromadka, of Prague. He had spent time in America after the communist takeover of Czechoslovakia, and had then returned to Communist-dominated Prague. He said to the reporters that he was happier in Prague than he had ever been in America. But why? Because being a Christian in America meant being assimilated to the materialistic American way of life, and that was far too easy an existence for a Christian. Being a Christian in Prague meant making a Christian confession in an atheist state at the risk of one's life, and living from day to day by faith in God alone.

There is no doubt that Lund arrested the complacent drift into an easy unity of spirit between those who were already like-minded, and brought the Churches sharply up against the double need to take non-theological factors into account and to re-examine the basis of faith on which alone real unity can be based.

When the World Council of Churches met for its second Assembly in 1954 in Evanston, Illinois, to consider the theme of 'Christ: the Hope of the World', attitudes such as those of Schlink and Hromadka were very much in the mind of the delegates. The Cold War was in progress, and the Christian attitude to Soviet totalitarianism and the use of the hydrogen bomb was under keen discussion everywhere in the West. Schlink addressed the Assembly on the same theme as at Lund, to meet with the same keen opposition from less apocalyptic and world-denying theologians. Urgent attention was given to the plight of the millions of refugees and the even greater number of those suffering from racial discrimination. For the first time at ecumenical gatherings the place of the laity in the ministry and mission of the Church was given an important place on the agenda.

It was not to be expected that consensus would easily be reached on the many controversial issues that were raised. But a consensus *did* painfully emerge in large areas of the Council's concerns. The conflict between those who said that the chief task of the Church is to prepare itself for the Second Coming of Christ and those who said that the Church must address itself to the problems of society in the name of the Christ who has already come was resolved in the Message of the Assembly to the Churches, in the words: 'We are not sufficient for these things. But Christ is sufficient. We do not know what is coming to us. But we know Who is coming. It is He who meets us every day and who will meet us at the end—Jesus Christ our Lord.'

The 'Faith and Order' section of the Assembly's Report was entitled 'Our Oneness in Christ and our Disunity as Churches'. It boldly asserted that 'the being and unity of Church belong to Christ, and therefore to its mission'. It ascribed our disunity to sin: 'do we not sin when we deny the sole lordship of Christ by claiming the vineyard for our own, by possessing "our church" for ourselves, by regarding our theology, order, history, nationality, etc., as our own "valued treasures", thus involving ourselves more and more in the separation of sin?' It reasserted the 'Lund principle', and called the Churches to listen more obediently to Scripture without denominational presuppositions, to consider frankly the influence of social and cultural differences on faith and order, and to learn afresh the implications of the one Baptism for sharing in the one Eucharist.

The delegates of the Eastern Orthodox Churches registered their dissent from many of these statements, and presented a report of their own on Faith and Order. Yet this fact did not prevent the Assembly from receiving the Report on 'Our Oneness in Christ and our Disunity as Churches', with its concluding sentences: 'At Amsterdam we said that we intend to stay together. Christ has kept us together. He has shown Himself again as our Hope. Emboldened by this Hope, we dedicate ourselves to God anew, that He may enable us to grow together.'

By the time that the Third Assembly met in New Delhi in 1961 the Russian Orthodox Church and the Polish Orthodox Church had decided to join the Eastern Orthodox Churches in full membership of the World Council. For the first time Pentecostal Churches—two of them, both from Latin America—became members; and eleven African Churches were added to the roll. The theme was 'Christ, the Light of the World', considered under the headings of Witness, Service and Unity. The Roman Catholic Church, as was now the custom, sent observers.

Without doubt the resultant statement on unity stood out at once from the other statements of the Assembly in directness and relevance, and shows considerable advance in these respects on earlier W.C.C. statements about this matter. 'We believe that the unity which is both God's will and his gift to his Church is being made visible as all in each place who are baptized into Jesus Christ and confess him as Lord and Saviour are brought by the Holy Spirit into one fully committed fellowship, holding the one apostolic faith, preaching the one Gospel, breaking the one bread, joining in common prayer, and having a corporate life reaching out in witness and service to all, and who at the same time are united with the whole Christian fellowship in all places and all ages in such wise that ministry and members are accepted by all, and that all can act and speak together as occasion requires for the tasks to which God calls his people.'

If this sentence had been shorter, or broken up into parts, it would, no doubt, have been even more effective than it was. But even as it was it commanded a sustained interest, and in many places a real attempt to put it into practice, of a kind that is rarely aroused by ecumenical pronouncements on a world scale. The phrase 'in each place' was interpreted by the document itself as meaning the local neighbourhood, other places where Christians work, worship and study together, and wider geographical areas such as states, provinces and nations. Thus the vision of Christian unity was brought down to earth from the starry world which visionaries inhabit, and localized in nations, towns, villages, factories and schools.

The Fourth World Conference on Faith and Order took place in Montreal in 1963. Perhaps because of the extreme discomfort and poor acoustics of the auditorium, but also, no doubt, for other reasons, this Conference did not mark the large step forward in the advance of unity that had been hoped for. But the 'observers' from the Roman Catholic Church, to everyone's delight, took a much more vigorous part in the proceedings than their official title indicated; and the Russian Orthodox Church was very powerfully represented. The entry of these globally important communions on the Faith and Order scene had the advantage and the disadvantage of bringing the 'old hands' at the Conference, who thought that many issues had been well settled in the past, back to a point rather near the beginning. This led to considerable conflict on the vexed question of the ministry, both in relation to the laity, whose place in the total ministry was now well recognized; and also in relation to the apostolic succession, interpreted in very different ways by 'catholics' and 'protestants'. The final report on 'The Redemptive Work of Christ and the Ministry of His Church' did, however, indicate a direction of thought which has been frequently taken since then in discussions of Church union: 'All ministry in the

THE WORLD IS THE SCENE

Church is rooted in the ministry of Christ himself, who glorified the Father in the power of the Holy Spirit. The special [i.e. the ordained] ministry reflects and serves the redemptive love of Christ. . . . Christ is High Priest; his Church is called to be the true priesthood in the world, holding out to all men the gift of the reconciliation which he has purchased, and offering up on behalf of all men both the sacrifice of praise, thanksgiving and obedience, and the prayer of penitence and intercession. That it may truly be so, the ministers are set for the priestly service of the Gospel in the midst of the priestly people.'

A brave attempt, also, was made at Montreal to break the theological impasse between 'protestants', who rely wholly on Scripture for the content of the Christian faith, and 'catholics', who put Tradition on a par with Scripture. The view was powerfully argued that 'Tradition', rightly understood, includes both Tradition as it is usually understood *and* Scripture. For the traditionary process, the process of handing down the Good News to the generations to come, began with the Apostles, and the Scripture was the first and normative product of it; the process went on, and resulted in the continuation of the 'Great Tradition' which is common to all Churches, and in the emergence of other traditions within particular Churches.

The event, however, which has remained most clearly in the minds of those who were present is a rally, of a then unprecedented kind, at which no one presided and no benediction was pronounced, and the last speaker was the Cardinal Archbishop of Montreal, Paul-Emile Léger, on 'We are one in Christ'. It was not so much what he said, but the fact that he was present to say it, that made the event unforgettable.

It is often alleged that theologians elaborate their teachings and Church leaders pursue their objectives irrespectively of the troubles through which the world is passing and in virtual ignorance of the directions in which human society is moving. This allegation is sometimes well-founded, but not in the case of those who came to Uppsala, Sweden, in July 1968, for the Fourth Assembly of the World Council of Churches to consider the theme: 'Behold, I make all things new.'

THE CHURCH IN OUR TIMES

The world was even more violently racked with troubles than usual. The civil war in Nigeria was being conducted with uncontrolled ferocity by apparently irreconcilable enemies; the U.S.A. was launched on its war in Vietnam which seared the conscience of every liberal-minded American; students were in militant revolt, from the Sorbonne to Berkeley, California, partly in the interest of extreme left-wing views, partly to improve their own conditions, partly to draw attention to the needs of the poor; the Civil Rights movement in America had burst into violence and Martin Luther King (who was scheduled to preach at the opening service of the Assembly) had been recently assassinated: in Czechoslovakia Dubcek had brought in his liberalizing reforms, and the world awaited the reaction of Moscow (which was not long delayed); and the more vigorous nations of the Third World were loudly articulating their desperate need for justice in the distribution of the world's resources.

There were also signs of hope. Pope John XXIII had brought a new spirit into the affairs of the Roman Catholic Church, and the Second Vatican Council had been held. There was every reason to think that Roman Catholics would join more and more in the concerted action and thought of Christians in every country, though the recent publication of the encyclical 'Humanae Vitae' on contraception had slightly damped down these expectations.

All these matters, and many others like them, were in the minds of the delegates to Uppsala. Their interpretation, and the action which the Council and the Churches and Christians should take in pursuance of this interpretation, provided the main content of the Assembly's deliberations, together with the recurrent issue of Christian unity. Being at Uppsala meant being caught up into a maelstrom of conflicting views, attitudes and (not least) passions, and trying to find a Christian way, however precarious, through the jungle of the world's perplexities.

Previous Assemblies had been mostly peopled and addressed (though somewhat less as time went on) by male white Western thinkers and administrators and those who willingly followed their guidance. The personnel of Uppsala

THE WORLD IS THE SCENE

was markedly different. There were more women than before, though they made up only 9 per cent of the whole. There were far more people from the Third World than before, though still only 31 per cent of the whole (and only 4 per cent from Latin America). Even the average age was lower, though only 39 per cent of the delegates were under fifty (and many more of these were from the developing countries than from Europe and America).

But more significant than numbers was the shift in interest and subjects of concern. It is not really an exaggeration to say that middle-aged European, American and British men were politely asked to take a back seat when the most vital issues of the Assembly were debated. When it had been made sufficiently clear that they were held to be largely responsible (in a representative capacity, of course) for the exploitation of the poor, the black, women and the young, they came back into prominence; and when the reports of the Assembly had to be drawn up and policy formulated, their help was warmly welcomed. There was a large international youth delegation which sought to make up for its lack of voting powers by vociferous protests and many distributed leaflets. There was a determined effort to obtain the election of a woman as one of the six Presidents of the Council for the ensuing septennium; this did not succeed, but to the general satisfaction Pauline Webb, the British Methodist, became one of the two Vice-Chairmen of the Central Committee.

Overriding all other themes were the predicament of the developing nations and the evil of racism in Southern Africa and elsewhere. President Kenneth Kaunda of Zambia, accompanied by an impressive bodyguard, Barbara Ward, James Baldwin and Lord Caradon placed the stark facts of economic and racial oppression before the Assembly, and their words coloured all the Assembly's reports on whatever subject. Out of its acute realization that the Church of Jesus Christ must be on the side of justice and the legitimate aspirations of the 'poor of the world', came the first beginnings of the 'Programme to Combat Racism' which caused so much controversy in later years.

But it is a travesty of Uppsala, encouraged by the almost

complete failure of the British Press to cover the Assembly except when controversial speeches on world politics were made, to suggest that the World Council had switched from religious to secular matters, from the pursuit of unity to leftist politics. In fact, there was sustained consideration of worship and the Christian style of life in the modern world; and the theology of the Church, its unity and its mission undergirded all its proceedings. What really happened was that those present who had not previously done so moved from an abstract, academic mode of theologizing to a mode which submitted Christian doctrine to the test of contemporary experience and held contemporary experience under the light of Christian truth.

Here is part of the Report on 'The Holy Spirit and the Catholicity of the Church' (which was drafted and re-drafted in the small hours of the morning, and thus painfully reached a real convergence of thought): 'In the agonizing arena of contemporary history—and very often among the members of the Churches—we see the work of demonic forces that battle against the rights and liberties of man, but we also see the activity of the life-giving Spirit of God. . . . Since Christ lived, died, and rose again for all mankind, catholicity is the opposite of all kinds of egoism and particularism . . . Diversity may be a perversion of catholicity but often it is a genuine expression of the apostolic vocation of the Church. . . . To the emphasis on 'all in each place' [from New Delhi] we would now add a fresh understanding of the unity of all Christians in all places. . . . The Church is bold in speaking of itself as the sign of the coming unity of mankind.'

The Church living 'in the shocks and turmoils of our times', the concept of 'diversity in unity', the unity of the Church as a foretaste and 'sign' of the unity of mankind—these themes were all to exercise considerable influence and engage much vigorous thought in the years after Uppsala. And the *Message of the Assembly* sums up its profoundest contribution to the Churches and the world: 'All men have become neighbours to one another. Torn by our diversities and tensions, we do not yet know how to live together. *But God makes new.* Christ wants his Church to foreshadow a renewed human community. Therefore we Christians will manifest our unity in Christ by entering into full fellowship with those of other races, classes, ages, religions and political convictions, in the place where we live. Especially we shall seek to overcome racism wherever it appears.'

The impression is sometimes created that ecumenical conferences consist of nothing (apart from the pleasant meeting of old friends from previous conferences) but complex arguments on theological and ecclesiastical issues, with agreements reached, perhaps, often late at night, in the corridors of power. The reality is that the experience of working with people of different races, nations and cultures, as well as from other communions, is liberating and broadening, bringing all kinds of intangible benefits to the countries and churches from which the participants come, especially if it is from a situation of persecution or isolation; and, still more, that however deep may be the satisfaction when a centuries-old misunderstanding is straightened out or a creative agreement is reached, the centre of each conference is its common worship. And most of those present usually place the high point of worship in the shared eucharist according to the rites of the host church, which invites all to communicate. On each such occasion some conference members cannot in conscience do so; this fact mars, but does not destroy, the unity which transcends the deepest-rooted differences.

Worship, in fact, forms the link between two expressions of ecumenism which have distinct historical origins—the theological and the liturgical. Indeed, the Liturgical Movement, or the Movement for Liturgical Renewal, not yet mentioned in this book was denominational in origin, and only became ecumenical in the course of its development. The history of the movement has not yet been fully chronicled or evaluated, but it seems to have arisen out of much discontent with the reiteration of traditional rites in which the congregation took little part in the Roman Catholic Church. The Benedictine monks of Solesmes, in the Department of Sarthe in France, and of Maria Laach, near Coblenz, in the Eifel, Germany, first of all applied themselves to the study of early and later liturgy, and then sought to re-mould eucharistic worship according to the pattern of the early Church, with a restored emphasis on the responses of the congregation. The movement spread from France and Germany to other parts of Continental Europe, and, somewhat later, to England. Pope Pius XII in 1947 allowed the use of the vernacular in all Sacraments except the eucharist, and this permission was later extended to all parts of the Eucharist, except for the Canon of the Mass.

After the Second World War the Movement began to attract the interest of other Churches, and at the same time it extended the range of its objectives. Gregory Dix's *The Shape of the Liturgy* (1943) had learnedly and vigorously reminded the Church of England of the fourfold pattern of the New Testament and early Christian eucharist—'he took the bread', 'he gave thanks', 'he broke it', 'he gave it to his disciples'—which had been somehow submerged in the Reformation liturgies and the Book of Common Prayer, and set on foot the process which led to the total revision of the Prayer Book rite. The 'Parish and People' group of clergy and laypeople fostered the replacement in many parishes of the conventional scheme of Sunday worship (early morning communion at which all communicate, followed by a Solemn Eucharist at which only the priest does so) by a Parish Communion (often followed by breakfast) at which everyone communicates. Then it became customary, where possible, for the celebrant (or, as he came to be called, the president) to stand behind the Holy Table; an offertory procession, in which members of the congregation bring in the elements, was widely introduced, and the ancient ceremony of the 'kiss of peace', which had been retained only in the Churches of the East, began to find its way back into services where experiments took place, within the established framework. Thus the eucharist was gradually transformed from a rather sombre occasion into a festive meal of the Christian family, where the remembered sorrows of the Passion were taken up into the joy of the Resurrection.

The Methodist Church, and to some extent the other Free Churches, became acutely aware of the frequent dullness and repetitiveness of their so-called extempore prayers and services, and groups within them took the Liturgical Movement very seriously. They encountered resistance to change, as the Roman Catholic and Anglican reformers also did, and some Free Churchmen feared the loss of their denominational identity. But the movement in Methodism went on, and resulted in the decision of the Methodist Conference to ask in 1963 for a complete re-writing of its 'Book of Offices'. The effect in the other Free Churches was largely confined to individuals and groups.

Liturgical revision thus got under way in England. It would certainly have been beneficial to the whole Church if the various Churches had worked together throughout the period of revision, and produced Orders of Service which could be used by all; but the ecumenical spirit and the now agreed principles of the Liturgical Movement ensured that a good deal of consultation took place; and the resultant services were at all major points remarkably similar. The Joint Liturgical Group in Britain, which was fully ecumenical, set to work in 1963 to look at the possibility of an agreed 'Daily Office', and an agreed rationalization of the 'Church's Year', wrote a lectionary and series of collects to follow its course. Its efforts were successful in producing what was required, but have not yet been universally accepted.

There was a time, not long ago, when Christians engaged in the study or conduct of worship did not think of consulting any but their own denominational experts and service books. Now the treasures of all denominations are open to each, and full advantage is being taken of this. Yet it is only when Churches work closely together in a particular district, or when an ecumenical conference, local, national or international, is in full swing, that Christians of all communions can fully appreciate what others have to contribute and be helped towards the enhancement of their own traditions.

Ecumenism, therefore, expresses itself in worship as well as in theology and church order. It can also express itself in community living. The most remarkable incarnation of ecumenism in an actual community is probably the protestant monastery of Taizé, near Cluny, in Southern France located there by Roger Schutz and Max Thurian in 1944. The Rule of

Taizé prescribes three offices a day and lay clothes (except at worship). The monks run a retreat house and a guest house, and organize a co-operative farm. Every year thousands of young men and women from many countries and more denominations come and camp in the grounds to share in worship, service to the nations and a great experience of communal happiness.

Not very different in spirit is the Community founded in 1938 by George MacLeod on the island of Iona in the Inner Hebrides. Here, laymen and ministers of the Church of Scotland, with many visitors from elsewhere, live together for periods of months, to prepare themselves for work in the industrial areas of Scotland, or overseas.

For many Christians not able to visit churches overseas or attend great conferences the impetus to ecumenical action since the Second World War has come from the Week of Prayer for Christian Unity (January 18th to 25th—the Feast of St Peter's Chair in Rome to the Feast of the Conversion of St Paul). This was introduced to the Christian world in general in 1939 by Paul Couturier, a French Roman Catholic priest. He taught his fellow-Christians to pray, not for the unity which they were sure was best for the Church, but for 'unity as and how Christ wills'. The Week of Prayer gained the approval and active support of the World Council of Churches and of nearly all Churches everywhere, and there cannot be very many Christians anywhere who are not at least invited to join in it.

It has perhaps now become clear that ecumenism as it has developed has become steadily more wide-embracing in its concerns—that it includes theology, practice and worship, and that it involves, or should involve, each local congregation in its setting of other congregations, each denomination in its setting of other denominations, each national Church or group of Churches in its setting of the world-wide Church, and the world-wide Church in its setting of human society. But in the chapters so far its scope has by no means been fully explored, for the largest Church of all, the Roman Catholic Church, has been rarely mentioned.

CHAPTER SIX

The Church of Rome Renewed

> Now is the winter of our discontent
> Made glorious summer by this sun of York.

THE CONTRAST between winter and summer is a not unsuitable analogy of the relations between the Roman Catholic Church and the non-Roman Catholic Churches before and after the advent of Pope John XXIII. The Council of Trent, which ended in 1563, had set an absolute and apparently permanent seal on the separation between the Church of the Roman obedience and the Churches which had rebelled against it. For four hundred years the only way for a non-Roman Catholic of establishing any relationship with the Church of Rome was by conversion, which meant the complete repudiation (in principle, at least) of his spiritual past.

No conversation on theological matters was permissible (though it must have taken place sometimes behind closed doors, or, in more recent days, during ecumenical conferences where Roman Catholic observers were present), and because communication was absent, misunderstanding was virtually complete. Catholics condemned Protestants for what they believed them to believe and practise, relying entirely on Catholic sources for their information: and Protestants did exactly the same the other way round. More effective still in prolonging the absolute separation were the deep emotions created and fostered by persecutions and martyrdoms, in the course of which the two sides probably suffered and sinned to an approximately equal degree. In the mind of all but the most enlightened Catholics, Protestants were nothing but damnable rebels, heretics and agents of Satan; in the minds of all but the most enlightened Protestants, Catholics were the superstitious assistants of the Bishop of Rome in the execution of his 'detestable enormities'. Of

THE CHURCH IN OUR TIMES

course, in ordinary social and personal life these bizarre convictions about the religious life of other Christians were modified by the discovery that those on the other side were often sincere and charitable people, contrary to all expectation. But no crisis in a family could be greater than the one which resulted when a son or daughter wished to marry an adherent of the 'other' faith.

All winters have genial periods, but the winter of Catholic–Protestant bitterness did not have very many until its later stages. When Giovanni Maria Mastai-Ferretti became Pope as Pius IX in 1846, his reputation for liberal ideas created hopes that he would encourage the discussion of contemporary ideas on science, politics and religion that were influential inside and outside the Church of Rome, and even that he might allow conversation with Protestant scholars. But the period of hope was brief. His failure to defend the temporal power of the Papacy against the tide of Italian nationalism seems to have persuaded him that its spiritual power was in danger also, and needed to be protected by an ultra-conservative theology. His *Syllabus of Errors*, published in 1864, reinforced by the accompanying Encyclical *Quanta Cura* and largely embodied in the Dogmatic Constitution of the First Vatican Council in 1870, condemned 'modern' thought under ten headings in eighty theses. Pantheism, Naturalism and Latitudinarianism, and other forms of rationalism, were predictably outlawed; Socialism and Communism went the same way. Bible Societies, societies of 'liberal' priests, and the whole world-view of contemporary theological liberalism came under an equal ban. The last thesis to be condemned was the one that stated that 'the Roman Pontiff can and ought to reconcile and adjust himself with progress, liberalism and modern civilization'.

The Pope had already, in 1854, defined the doctrine of the Immaculate Conception of the Virgin Mary as a matter of faith for all Catholics. The definition further alienated most Protestants, but did little more than ratify what was already a universal belief among Catholics. More controversial was the decision of the First Vatican Council in 1870 to promulgate the dogma of Papal Infallibility, favoured by Pius IX. This has

THE CHURCH OF ROME RENEWED

often been misunderstood by Protestants to say more than it actually does, but it does say that 'the Roman Pontiff, when he speaks *ex cathedra*, that is, when in discharge of the office of pastor and doctor of all Christians, by virtue of his supreme Apostolic authority, he defines a doctrine regarding faith and morals to be held by the universal Church, by the divine assistance promised to him in blessed Peter, is possessed of that infallibility with which the divine Redeemer willed that his Church should be endowed for defining doctrine regarding faith and morals, and that therefore such definitions of the Roman Pontiff are irreformable of themselves, and not from the consent of the Church'.

The decree on infallibility, on which it seemed impossible for the Roman Catholic Church ever to go back, undoubtedly widened an already immense gap between that Church and the rest of Christendom. It also excluded, either immediately or subsequently, a number of Roman Catholic scholars who could not in conscience foreswear their Biblical and historical enquiries—the most notable being Alfred Loisy (1857–1940), perhaps the most brilliant (and also one of the most radical) scholars of the age, who was excommunicated in 1907.

From the point of view of Anglicans the severest blow to any hope of reunion with Rome was administered by the encyclical of Pope Leo XIII in 1896, *Apostolicae Curae*, which condemned the orders of Anglican bishops and priests as invalid, both because of the form of the Anglican Ordinal and because the Church of England, as is shown by its Ordinal, does not have the intention of conferring upon priests the power to offer sacrifice. A protest against this ruling issued by the Archbishops of Canterbury and York was of no avail.

Thus the Church of Rome entered the twentieth century in splendid isolation. But the isolation was not quite complete. Baron Friedrich von Hügel, of German and Scottish parentage, who was a friend and admirer of Loisy, strove hard to build bridges of spiritual communion and theological understanding between Catholics and Protestants. His book *The Mystical Element of Religion* and his *Essays and Addresses* helped greatly to this end. He was trusted as a spiritual counsellor by men and women of all types of Christian faith; he was never excommunicated, nor were any of his writings formally condemned. He taught that the Institutional, the Intellectual and the Mystical were the three necessary constituents of religion, and he urged his friends on both sides of the Catholic-Protestant argument to pay proper respect to each of the three.

In 1921, 1923 and 1925 Lord Halifax, an eminent leader of the Anglo-Catholics in the Church of England, arranged, with Cardinal Mercier, Archbishop of Malines, a series of conversations between Roman Catholic and Anglican theologians designed to reconcile the Church of England with the Church of Rome on doctrinal matters. Agreement was reached by those present on giving to the Pope the primacy of honour, on the Real Presence of Christ in the eucharistic elements and on the reality of the sacrifice of the Mass. But in 1928 Pope Pius XI, in the encyclical *Mortalium Animos*, forbade Roman Catholics to take part in reunion movements, such as the World Faith and Order Movement, and implicitly condemned the Malines Conversations. The Conversations, of course, did not in any case carry authority from either Church.

But Mercier was by no means alone within the Roman Catholic Church in his aspirations towards Christian unity. In 1924, Karl Adam, Professor in the Catholic Faculty of Theology in Tübingen, where he had frequent contact with his colleagues in the Evangelical Theological Faculty, published a book which was translated into English under the title *Catholicism*, and many Protestants were heard to say that if they were ever to be converted to Roman Catholicism, Adam had described the version of it to which they would give their allegiance. In the book Adam stressed the spiritual rather than the institutional significance of the Roman Catholic Church's structure, and suggested that Protestants, though they did not yet belong to the body of the Church, yet did belong to its soul.

During the Nazi period German Roman Catholics in many cases took as firm a stand against the interference of the State with the Church as did the Confessional Protestants. Karl

THE CHURCH OF ROME RENEWED

Adam attacked elements in Nazi ideology, and Cardinal Faulhaber, of Munich, criticized the Nazis with considerable courage. Thus a common cause was invisibly formed between the two main kinds of Christian in Germany. After the Second World War, however, there were few signs that this had taken place. Moreover, the unyielding attitude of the Papacy was again shown in its treatment of the writings of the French savant, Teilhard de Chardin. On palaeontology and other scientific subjects he was free to publish what he wished; but his theological writings were banned until after his death in 1955.

In the *Phenomenon of Man*, and later books, Teilhard expounds the divine process of creation and salvation as evolutionary. The beginning of life, the emergence of man, and the development of rationality and self-consciousness in man (at which point man himself begins to take a hand in his own development) are the early stages of man's progress into the 'noosphere', where all things and persons human will be gathered up into Christ and God will be all in all. It has to be admitted that this theology takes little account of the doctrine of the Fall of Man, and is in any case, perhaps, unduly optimistic about man's steady progress. Yet the book has provided a frame of reference and a coherence of thought which has been found immensely helpful by Catholics and Protestants alike, since it points always towards the unity of all things and all people in Christ, looking beyond our present differences of theology and culture.

In 1950 Pope Pius XII, in response to myriad appeals from the faithful in many parts of the world, defined as a matter of faith, and therefore infallibly, the doctrine that the Blessed Virgin Mary 'having fulfilled the course of her earthly life, was taken up in body and soul to heavenly glory'. The doctrine, not to be found in the New Testament, scarcely known in the early Church, but formulated by Gregory of Tours at the end of the sixth century and recognized as a 'probable opinion' by several of the great Schoolmen, was regarded by Roman Catholics in general as the logical climax of the other beliefs of the Church about the Virgin Mary. To most non-Roman Catholics it seemed the absolute negation of Biblical and historical scholarship, and its definition another unwarrantable assertion of Papal supremacy.

But the long winter was, incredibly, almost over, and after a very short spring,* the summer came. Angelo Giuseppe Roncalli, having shown a modest but real capacity for scholarship, an open mind towards developments in France where Parisian priests were temporarily allowed to work in secular industrial occupations (the 'Worker Priests'), but no particular interest in ecumenical activities, was elected Pope in 1958 as John XXIII at the age of seventy-seven. He was perhaps thought of simply as a 'caretaker' until some more distinguished prelate showed himself to be capable of the Supreme Pontificate. But it became immediately clear that he had a spirit, a mind and a policy of his own. Almost at once he created twenty-three new cardinals, in order to make the College more internationally representative, and ninety days after his enthronement he announced his intention of summoning the Twenty-first Ecumenical Council. Three and a half years of intensive preparation were needed before the Council could actually meet, and this was carried out with the utmost thoroughness. The Council opened in the Vatican on October 11th, 1962, and, after four sessions charged with momentous deliberations, closed on December 8th, 1965. Pope John died between the first and second sessions, in 1963; but his stamp remained on all the discussions and decisions of the Council, known to history as Vatican II.

It is not to be supposed that Pope John was the 'onlie begetter' of the new spirit and of the multitude of new ideas that emerged at the Council, or that those who took the lead at every level of Church life in promoting and developing the 'aggiornamento' (the renewal of the Church and of the presentation of its message) which was the keynote of Pope John's programme and of the work of the Council, were suddenly converted to a new point of view by the advent of John. For many years previously in various parts of the

* One of the signs of spring was the *Prayers of Life* (1961) of Michel Quoist, who taught many Catholics and Protestants by his book that God speaks in and through the most ordinary events and feelings.

THE CHURCH OF ROME RENEWED

Roman Catholic Church there had been the steady growth of creative ideas, of constructive (and sometimes caustic) criticism of the old ways of thinking, speaking and acting, and of a new attitude to non-Roman Catholic Christians. But this had taken place invisibly, or when it had emerged into the open it had been suppressed. What Pope John did was to release the dammed-up stream of ideas and give his blessing to the new spirit, and thereby, at the same time, to create and inspire a new generation of pastors and theologians who were able and willing to work out the contemporary significance of their Church's traditions, and simultaneously to welcome new ways of thinking from non-Roman Catholic, and even secular, sources. The Council in many cases, of course, came up with ideas that seemed to Roman Catholics in the main to be highly original, but had in fact been familiar to non-Roman Catholics for many years, and in some cases ever since the Reformation, but even these basically old notions were infused with a new flexibility and a new dynamic.

The ultimate purpose of the Council, in the mind of John XXIII at least, was the reunion of all Christians, but no one knew better than he and his advisers that the way to that was long and arduous, and that a great number of massive obstacles had to be removed patiently, one by one.

The pronouncements of the Council (for none of which was infallibility or definitiveness claimed) which most clearly promoted the cause of Christian unity were those on 'the Church', 'Divine Revelation', 'Ecumenism', 'the Apostolate of the Laity', and 'Religious Freedom'.

On the Church, 'Lumen Gentium' (called this from the first words in the official, Latin, version) takes up a deeply pastoral point of view—indeed, one of its major contentions is that the Church continues the work of the Good Shepherd—and lays equal emphasis on the Church as the people of God as on the Church as the Body of Christ. Much attention is given to the role of bishops within the Church, but chiefly in order to point out that not his power and authority, but his functions of teaching, sanctifying and governing the People of God, mark the true bishop of the flock of Christ; and that the bishops are responsible for the leadership of the

THE CHURCH IN OUR TIMES

Church not as individuals, but collectively—according to the 'principle of collegiality'.

'Among the principal duties of bishops', says Lumen Gentium, 'the preaching of the Gospel occupies an eminent place.' Therefore, it is argued, 'in matters of faith and morals, the bishops speak in the name of Christ, and the faithful are to accept their teaching and adhere to it with a religious assent of soul'. Such assent must also be shown in a special way to the teaching authority of the Pope, even when he is not speaking *ex cathedra*. When he *does* speak *ex cathedra*, 'to proclaim by a definitive act some doctrine of faith or morals', his definitions are irreformable, and he is exercising his charism (his special gift) of infallibility. So far Vatican II repeats Vatican I. But then Vatican II goes on to say that 'the infallibility promised to the Church resides also in the body of bishops when that body exercises supreme teaching authority with the successor of Peter', and it is evident from the main tenor of the whole document on the Church that the Council hoped and expected that future definitive pronouncements on doctrine and morals would be made not by the Pope alone (though he is entitled to do so), but by the Pope speaking with the college of bishops.

In the Dogmatic Constitution 'on Divine Revelation' there is a strong emphasis, endearing to Protestants, on the duty of all the faithful to study the Scriptures, and a virtual acceptance of modern methods of historical and Biblical criticism (if not carried to extremes). The Bible, it is stated, contains divine revelation in the form of the written record of the apostolic testimony. This record was given to a living community, and has been interpreted and re-expressed continuously within that community by the succession of bishops under the guidance of the Holy Spirit. Thus the Scriptures, tradition and the 'magisterium' (the teaching office) of the Church are engaged in constant interplay, to the instruction, building up and sending into the world of Christians in every generation.

In some ways the most remarkable thing about the Decree 'on Ecumenism' is that it exists at all. Before the time of John XXIII it was almost inconceivable that such a document would ever be issued. But much of its content is remarkable also. It greets the members of the separated 'Churches and Communities' with respect and affection as brothers in the Lord; they have been baptized, and thus 'brought into a certain, though imperfect, communion with the Catholic Church', and 'incorporated into Christ'. In these 'Ecclesial Communities', 'some, even very many' of 'the most significant elements which together go to build up and give life to the Church itself' are to be found: the written word of God; the life of grace; faith, hope and charity—though these communities have not preserved the genuine and total reality of the Eucharistic mystery because they lack the sacrament of order.

This Decree marked the full entrance of the Roman Catholic Church into the Ecumenical Movement, and made possible a large range of shared acts of worship, theological consultation and social activities between Roman Catholics and the rest of Christendom all over the world. There has been and can be no turning back on that. Not every problem by any means was solved by the Decree; but a positive common approach to every divisive issue was opened up by it.

The Dogmatic Constitution 'on the Church' deliberately includes the laity in the mission of the People of God—a self-evidently proper inclusion in the eyes of Protestants, but not an obvious derivative from the traditions of Roman Catholicism. The point was taken up and expanded both for theory and for practice in the Decree 'on the Apostolate of the Laity', which goes a long way towards reiterating the traditional Protestant doctrine of the corporate priesthood of all believers. By virtue of baptism and living union with Christ, and nourished by active participation in the sacred liturgy, laypeople do their work in the world, live their family life and carry out deeds of charity and service to the Church and the community at large, as apostles of Christ; and 'the perfect example of this type of spiritual and apostolic life is the most Blessed Virgin Mary, Queen of the Apostles'.

It could here be said—as also with some truth about the Decree on the Laity—that in the 'Declaration on Religious Freedom' the Roman Catholic Church was simply catching up with other Christians who had long proclaimed their allegiance to the principle of tolerance. But certainly it cleared the air on an issue which had long embittered Catholic-Protestant relationships, by repudiating the double standard by which Roman Catholics had claimed from secular states freedom for the Church when Catholics were in a minority, and a position of privilege for the Church, and the power to suppress others, when they were in a majority.

In addition to these largely 'ecumenical' matters the Council covered a wide range of attitudes and practices within the life of its own Church, with the stress always on 'renewal'; it concerned itself also with a fresh approach to many national and social problems; and it put right a longstanding and brutal injustice, which had for centuries been the source of anti-Semitism in many Christian countries, by declaring that 'what happened in the passion of Jesus Christ cannot be blamed upon all the Jews then living, nor upon the Jews of today'. The Council went on to deplore 'the hatred, persecution and displays of anti-Semitism directed against the Jews at any time and from any source'. It is a matter of deep shame to every Christian that the charge of deicide against the Jews had never been formally withdrawn until this moment, and of gratitude to God that the charge can never be made again with a shred of ecclesiastical blessing.

As a symbol of his ultimate aim of reconciliation and union, Pope John had invited distinguished observers from the other main Churches of the world to attend the Council. They were warmly greeted and splendidly cared for when they came, their comments at the time and subsequently were asked for and treated respectfully, and they were unanimous in recognizing the Council as a genuinely epoch-making event in the history of the Church.

The expositors of the Council's Constitutions and Decrees, both inside and outside the Roman Catholic Church, have been numerous. Most influential in Roman Catholic circles is perhaps Professor Karl Rahner, of Munich, notable not only for his attempt to reinterpret the theology of St Thomas Aquinas in modern terms, but also for his wish to show to all Christians how Roman Catholics could be open to Christian

THE CHURCH OF ROME RENEWED

insights from every source without repudiating the traditional teaching of the Church.

Hans Küng, Professor in the Catholic Faculty of Tübingen, has expounded the message of the Council from a different standpoint. In a series of books on justification (where he shows an understanding of Martin Luther until recently very rare in the Roman Catholic Church), the Church and its structures, infallibility and reunion, he has expressed many radical criticisms of his Church before and after the Council, and more recently summoned it to the full implementation of the Council's call for renewal and its quest for reunion. In the book in which he has brought together the essential points of his life's teaching, *On being a Christian*, written especially with the problems and needs of contemporary man in mind, he sets out a coherent view of Christian faith and practice which can be acceptable to Catholics and non-Catholics alike. But he does this, as many Catholics would say, at the cost of casting doubt on traditional Catholic doctrine about miracles, the Person of Christ, the nature of the Church and infallibility; and he warmly supports the ordination of women. Not surprisingly, his book is regarded with suspicion in orthodox Roman Catholic circles. He has been called to Rome to answer for some of his beliefs, and has failed to appear. Yet he confesses himself a devout member of the Roman Catholic Church from which he has no intention of departing.

No one would ascribe to Pope Paul VI, elected in 1963, the same clarity and simplicity of vision that were granted to his predecessor. He could be said, however, to have a wider grasp of the consequences involved by his predecessor's policy. This is no doubt why the following-up of Vatican II has been for the most part cautious and gradual. He had given more heed to the conservative members of the Curia than John did, and at one point he seemed even to be re-creating the wintry scene of the past. This was when in 1968 he issued the encyclical *Humanae Vitae*, condemning all forms of contraception except the 'rhythm method'. It is widely supposed that in doing this he rejected the advice of the majority of those whom he had appointed to the Papal Commission on the subject. He took his stand unwaveringly on 'natural law', and rejected not only all 'artificial' contraception but also abortion in any circumstance and all forms of sterilization. It cannot be known, of course, how many Roman Catholics have disobeyed his advice and how many hope for the reversal of the teaching of the Encyclical by a future Pope.

Yet he has also promoted the reform of the liturgy and its use in the vernacular, as Vatican II advised, and in the process welcomed the assistance of non-Roman Catholic scholars; he has cancelled the anathemas pronounced in 1054 on the Orthodox Churches of the East, visited the World Council of Churches and welcomed the Archbishop of Canterbury to Rome. It is with his blessing that conversations have taken place with other world-wide Christian Communions, notably the Anglicans and the Methodists, on the Ministry, the Eucharist and Authority.

Of the statements which have appeared, those issued by the Anglican-Roman Catholic International Commission (A.R.C.I.C.) have received the greatest publicity. In each case the authors have striven to indicate agreement on the central matters under discussion, and in this they have frequently succeeded, although their critics suggest that at certain crucial points they gloss over remaining differences—as when they say, in the Canterbury Statement of 1973, that the ministry of the ordained 'is not an extension of the common priesthood but belongs to another realm of the gifts of the Spirit', without saying what that realm is.

On the Eucharist, the Windsor Statement (1971) shows the authors to be at one on the Real Presence: 'the elements are not mere signs; Christ's body and blood become really present and are really given. But they are really present and given in order that, receiving them, believers may be united in communion with Christ the Lord.' The long-vexed question of transubstantiation is in 1971 relegated to a footnote, 'as a term used by Roman Catholics to denote the reality of the eucharistic presence and not as implying as of necessity any particular view of how that presence is brought about or what its metaphysical character is'.

The third of the Statements, the Venice Statement on 'Authority' (1977) is particularly marked by a characteristic which is to be found to some degree in the two earlier ones also. It is assumed, without argument, that the developments of belief and practice which took place in the episcopal communions of the Church are the only ones that have the sanction of the Holy Spirit, and that they have that sanction beyond a doubt. Thus the authority which accrued historically to the See of Rome is not ultimately to be questioned, though it may have to be re-interpreted. Thus, also, the Protestant claim to have reached a truer understanding of Scripture and to have reinstated the New Testament teaching on authority and ministry at the Reformation is simply passed over, instead of becoming a fruitful field for ecumenical discussion. Yet the emphasis in the Statement on the pastoral aspect of authority and on the cooperation of the priesthood and the laity is welcome to all. The problem of infallibility is reserved for later consideration.

The Roman Catholic-Methodist statements on Eucharist and Ministry (the one on Authority is still in course of preparation) adopt a different method. They expound the large—unexpectedly large—areas of agreement between the two Churches, and then set out the matters on which disagreement still persists. On the Eucharist, the Real Presence is asserted, but it is acknowledged that the sacrificial character of the liturgical action is differently interpreted by the two Churches. On the Ministry, much agreement on priesthood is recorded, but the nature of the difference between the universal priesthood and the priesthood of the individual is agreed to be still in dispute. 'We both see the central act of the ordained ministry as presiding at the eucharist in which the ministry of word, sacrament and pastoral care is perfected. Roman Catholics affirm that in the way the ordained minister represents Christ to the body of the faithful he is a priest in a sense in which other Christians are not.'

None of these inter-confessional statements has received the official approval of the Churches involved. It is wise to see them, not as definitive statements of agreed doctrine, but as important stages in the progress towards Christian reunion for which Pope John XXIII prayed and worked.

Good can be brought out of evil, but evil sometimes comes

out of good. Roman Catholic participation in the Ecumenical Movement has had two disadvantageous effects which are fortunately likely to be temporary. The progress of Christian unity in particular countries has sometimes been held up by World Confessional bodies, such as the Lutheran World Federation and the World Methodist Council, who have seen more good in world-wide confessionalism than in local, national or regional unity. The Roman Catholic Church is the largest and most powerful World Confessional body of all, and its presence on the ecumenical stage has made World Confessionalism outside the Roman Catholic Church a more powerful ingredient in the general ecumenical situation than it was before. This is not all to the good, since it may foster the dream of a World Methodist or a World Lutheran Church.

Second, in England a large, important and theologically-convinced body of Anglicans has always cherished the hope of reunion with Rome and made this the principal object of their ecumenical efforts—in fact, to some of them the very word 'ecumenical' means this and only this. Now that Rome herself has turned in the direction of other Churches, and not least towards the Church of England, such Anglicans are understandably very eager not to allow their Church to be committed to anything that would endanger this hoped-for rapprochement with Rome. Many of them fear that union, or even intercommunion, with the English Free Churches would do just that, and this fear has gradually become a serious factor in the Anglican approach to reunion in England. It could even be said that for some Anglicans the hope of reunion with Rome, distant though it must undoubtedly be, has banished all thought of a wider reunion from their minds.

Yet Rome herself cannot be held responsible for these developments, which, indeed, she sometimes seeks to correct. Unofficially, leading English Roman Catholics gave support to the Anglican-Methodist Scheme in 1971; officially, in later years, the Ecumenical Commission has encouraged the non-Roman Catholic Churches to go forward to visible unity, seeing in this no bar to the greater reunion, though there have been pronouncements by individual bishops in the opposite direction, as by the influential Bishop Christopher Butler in May 1978.

The real situation between the Roman Catholic Church and the other Churches of Christendom then is this: the Roman Catholic Church and the Orthodox Churches of the East are making tentative approaches to each other, and some of the very formidable barriers between them—such as the question of the primacy of the Pope—are being slowly eroded. The Roman Catholic Church has acknowledged that the Church of England has a relation to itself different from that of the other Churches of the Reformation, since it has retained the historic episcopacy; on many important matters of doctrine agreement is being earnestly sought for and in some matters reached; yet the recognition of Anglican Orders and the establishment of full communion are not in immediate prospect—as Cardinal Hume of Westminster made very clear in January 1978 in response to the Archbishop of Canterbury's request to him for full communion between the two Churches, by saying that such communion is not a means to organic union but the consummation of it. Between the Roman Catholic Church and the other Churches of the Reformation active and friendly conversations are proceeding, ancient misunderstandings are being removed, and the question of full communion is at least being discussed. Meanwhile it is the policy of the Roman Catholic Church to encourage all movements towards unity, whether with itself or between non-Roman Catholic Churches, in the hope that they will all contribute to the overall pattern of unity that one day will emerge. This could well be the policy of all other Churches, as it already is of some.

In the narrower field of local co-operation in England, which is what concerns most English Christians most nearly, there is much goodwill, but also great unevenness in the putting of this goodwill into practice. Roman Catholic congregations are often members of local Councils of Churches and co-operate fully in every matter short of eucharistic worship; in other areas the old suspicions die more slowly.

Yet there is an almost universal acknowledgement that of

all the events which have taken place in the Catholic Church during the period covered by this book, the Second Vatican Council must take pride in achievement and promise. By it the past has been redeemed and the present filled with life and hope.

CHAPTER SEVEN

Uncertain Britain in the Sixties

WE HAVE brought ecumenical developments on the world stage to the end of the sixties and beyond. Now we must come back to Britain and trace the developments here. Once again in the sixties the Church was faced with a new situation, and each element in it seemed to make the work of the Church more difficult. The strangest thing about that turbulent decade was the widely held notion that the Western world had entered a period of settled prosperity. There were, of course, signs that Britain had shaken off many of the effects of the Second World War and of the ill-judged Suez enterprise in the fifties; there was still full employment, money was available for many useful projects, notably new schools and the development of universities; and ordinary people enjoyed a degree of wealth and comfort previously undreamed-of. The temptation to believe Harold Macmillan's 'we've never had it so good' was therefore strong, and the temptation to adopt a crude materialism even stronger. Across the North Sea West Germany was in a similarly prosperous condition. Across the Atlantic the United States seemed unassailably affluent—and the British had become accustomed to hope (or fear) that what America has today, Britain will have tomorrow.

This widespread prosperity was ultimately shown to rest on very weak foundations, and soon felt to be threatened. Meanwhile the consciousness of Western affluence gave birth to a widespread movement of protest in other parts of the world, sometimes militant, always angry. For this was the time when the developing nations of Asia and Africa, having gained their independence, became painfully aware of the smallness of their resources, and of the long history of oppression and exploitation by their colonial masters; not unnaturally they used the means now open to them, at the United

Nations and elsewhere, of making their grievances and their urgent needs known on a world scale; their cries of protest were taken up by those who believed themselves oppressed in the countries of the First World also, blacks in America, women in most English-speaking countries, students in all countries.

The case of the students was complex. Those who were not students thought of them as an especially privileged section of the community, with the chance to postpone the necessity of honest work for three or more years with all expenses paid. The students (including those of the theological kind) saw the matter very differently, believing themselves to be deprived of their right to earn large salaries like everyone else while they were submitted to a discipline, in the formulation of which they had no say, calculated to make them the convenient and conditioned agents of the capitalist system. At least, enough of them felt like this to mount large demonstrations and sit-ins against most forms of authority. But mixed up with this intense feeling of personal grievance was a genuine imaginative sympathy with 'the poor of the world' in Asia and Africa, the undeserving victims of Western colonialism and (its successor) paternalism. It was sometimes hard to discern whether a 'demo' was designed to remove the hardships of the students demonstrating, or those of the oppressed peoples across the world.

The Cuban crisis, which nearly brought the world to nuclear destruction, the murder of John Kennedy (who was one of the few hopes of the liberals to hold real power), the Sharpeville massacre, the shootings at Kent State University, the assassination of Martin Luther King, and, in a lower key, the Profumo scandal in Britain, served only, in the mind of the protesters, to show the rottenness of the established order, the corruption of governments, and the powerlessness of individuals and minorities. Thus outward affluence had fostered protest, and protest pinpointed deep confusion everywhere.

The sexual revolution, contemporaneous with all this, and the emergence in the West of the 'permissive society', resulted as much from the invention of the contraceptive pill as from any other single event; but this could not have had the effect it did without a general revolt against authority (tellingly exemplified by the BBC's weekly satire 'That was the week that was'), the general questioning of moral values, the influence of writers like Kenneth Tynan and Kingsley Amis and the general atmosphere of plays and films. Permissiveness has its good and bad sides: it means, presumably, that certain restraints, which we can now see to be indefensible, on the discussion of sex, on proper sex education, on social relations between the sexes, on literary expression, and on personal freedom to choose one's own way of life, were removed; it also came to mean, more and more, that all other restraints on sexual behaviour, including types of it hitherto regarded as deviant, and on the publication of pornography, were removed as well. Thus public confusion was accompanied by basic changes in private standards—so that, among other things, the normal difficulty which parents and children have in understanding each others' values was dangerously increased. It is impossible yet to assess the advantages and disadvantages of permissiveness for personal wholeness and social cohesion.

All this is rehearsed simply in order to indicate the considerable changes in the climate of society of which the Churches in the West were challenged to take account, though they sometimes refused to do so. Nor indeed were the Churches themselves by any means immune from the movements of the times. We have seen already how deeply the Assembly of the World Council of Churches in Uppsala (1968) was influenced by the world-situation. The national situation in Britain made a sharp impact on the life and thought of its Churches, even though many Christians attempted to live and think as if these things were not happening at all, and some others deliberately rebelled against them and repudiated them wholly.

The event which stabbed the semi-aware Christians into full awareness of the chaotic situation was the publication in 1963 of *Honest to God*, by John Robinson, Bishop of Woolwich. The fact that John Robinson was a bishop no doubt increased the furore that resulted: other people, not bishops, had expressed similar sentiments to his, and not been noticed. The appearance of a front-page article by Robinson in the *Observer*, called 'Our Image of God must go', on the Sunday before the book came out (this was quite fortuitous, resulting from the editor's urgent need to find a piece to replace one that had not been sent in), helped to create immense public interest at a time when the intelligentsia had mostly decided that religion was finished.

Honest to God is a confused and confusing book, in tune with the times. It was written (as is admitted) very quickly, without any expectation of mass circulation. It pursues various interesting ideas, quotes various interesting people, and then seems to backtrack and contradict itself. But its readers, whether they follow the arguments or not, are left with the overall impression that orthodox ideas of God are outdated for modern man, that God is neither 'up there', nor 'out there', but perhaps 'in the depths of our being'; that Christian morality is suspect; that, the 'supernatural' is 'out'; that love is God, and that Jesus Christ, the 'man for others', is a window through whom God can be seen.

Whether Robinson intended to give currency to all these ideas is not quite certain; what is quite certain is that no responsible Christian teacher for centuries has taught that God is 'up there' or 'out there'; that many had put out ideas about God 'in the depths of our being' (an idea which seems to go back to Meister Eckhart in the fourteenth century); that Christian morality (sexual and other) certainly needs re-examining; and that the conception of Jesus as the 'man for others' is a stimulating though not an exclusive one. We must surely conclude that Robinson's achievement was to release to the public what theologians had known for a long time (but had somehow not passed on to the people, and often not to the clergy), and to launch various unfamiliar (though sometimes dubious) ideas at the same time. What shocked many Christians, enlightened a great number. And there was an element of emancipation in the process since many people felt that they now had episcopal permission to believe what they had wanted to believe for a long time.

Robinson drew overdue attention to German thinkers

whose works had taken a long time to become well known in England, Dietrich Bonhoeffer above all. Bonhoeffer's early death at the hands of the Nazis had prevented him from bringing his thought to its systematic conclusion. But many of his published works are full of suggestive ideas, often cryptic in expression, which have moved others to carry them much further. He believed that modern man, because of his intellectual achievements, especially in the realm of science, had 'come of age', and that 'God is teaching us that we must live as men who can get along very well without him' (quoted with great approval in *Honest to God*). We live in a world in which we no longer have to fall back upon God as an explanation of what happens or as a means of getting done what we want to be done. We are now independent of God and can do what we want to do by our own knowledge and efforts. But this does not mean that God does not exist; on the contrary, 'the God who makes us live in this world without using him as a working hypothesis is the God before whom we are ever standing. Before God and with him we live without God.'

So to live without God is God's gift to us; and to live thus is the essence of faith. Religion, which is the attempt to enlist God on our side, is a survival of superstition; 'cheap grace', the opposite of real grace, is what we attempt to buy from God by the performance of religious acts. Bonhoeffer's own life and death, his reflections on the great themes of Christian theology, and his *Letters from Prison*, form the clearest possible expression of his own total commitment to God from which his theology springs.

Paul Tillich (1886–1965), who was forced to leave Germany when Hitler came to power, and then taught in New York, Harvard and Chicago, was for a period by far the most popular lecturer in theology throughout America, and the most quoted thinker in Protestant student circles throughout the world. This was because he possessed a particularly sympathetic understanding of the thought-processes of the intelligent young in the West. He by no means despised the dogmas of Christianity, nor the traditional modes of understanding and expressing them. But he deliberately set out to re-interpret them in the language of contemporary culture, in spite of the dangers, which he fully recognized, of doing so. So 'God' becomes 'the Ground of our being'—not 'the *depths* of our being' (which are in us), but that in which all being subsists and on which it depends, which is yet personally related to us as persons. 'Faith in God' becomes our total allegiance to 'the object of our ultimate concern' (which may indeed not be conceived *by us* as God in any sense, so that we may be 'justified by faith' if we give ourselves to an ideal, without being Christians at all). But overarching all is his thought of God as gracious, forgiving us and accepting us as we have no right to be forgiven or accepted, and inviting us to 'accept that we are accepted'.

Rudolf Bultmann (1884–1976) was Professor in Marburg for thirty years until his retirement in 1951. He was by original interest a New Testament scholar, but he carried the insights gained from this discipline into many other fields of thought. He was an early exponent of the Form Criticism of the Gospels, giving meticulous attention to the 'frame' of words or events in which each deed and saying and story of Jesus was remembered, handed on, and incorporated into the evangelists' narrative. He came steadily to the conclusion, on the basis of this study, that what we know for certain about Jesus is very little—simply that he preached the Kingdom of God, called for personal decision and was crucified, and that those who chose to trust in him before and after his death received the gift of new life, which they described by saying that they were 'risen with Christ'.

He also claimed, both from his historical studies and from the effort to preach the Gospel to modern man (and he was no mean preacher), that the whole New Testament was written in the terminology of the three-decker universe (heaven, earth and hell)—a view of the world, or 'myth', which no longer has any meaning for us today. It must therefore be 'de-mythologized' and its essential meaning conveyed in other language. The language he came to choose was that of Martin Heidegger, the existentialist philosopher who spoke (as Bultmann did not speak) of living 'in the absence of God', but also distinguished 'inauthentic' existence (living by rules and conventions derived from other people or from society around us) from 'authentic' existence (living one's own life in conscious freedom from the imposed or accepted will of others). Bultmann took up this distinction and affirmed that 'authentic' existence was the gift of God to those who accepted the Gospel preached by Jesus and entered on his 'resurrection life'. To live 'authentically' is to be open to God and to other people, to be free from fear and prejudice; to make and carry through one's own free choices.

Robinson in *Honest to God* popularized some of the ideas of these three thinkers, but had neither the time nor the space to do them justice. Two much more solid works with the same general tendency came from America, one almost simultaneously with and the other just after the publication of his sensational little book—*The Secular Meaning of the Gospel*, by Paul van Buren (1963) and *The Secular City*, by Harvey Cox (1965). Both the titles include the word 'secular' in the new and particular sense which was then coming into fashion. The authors were not concerned simply to emphasize the old truism (not even yet fully accepted by all Christians) that the Bible makes no distinction between the sacred and the secular; they were declaring their conviction that the Gospel is not concerned solely, if indeed at all, with 'the things that are unseen and eternal'—the life to come, the essential nature of God and of reality—but with this world, this *seculum*, in which we live, and of which our knowledge and control are steadily increasing.

Van Buren was very conscious of the attacks made on theological thinking by modern linguistic philosophers who said that it was hard to attach a determinate meaning to the word 'God', since it referred to a being who was alleged to be beyond our experience of the physical world. In answer to this he was willing to interpret 'God' in terms of human history and ethics, on the ground that God has told us all that we can understand about himself in Jesus, and with this we must be content. Statements about God are thus really statements about man. Christians, by saying 'Jesus is Lord', 'express a particular perspective upon life and history', derived from the teaching and career of Jesus; and they are enabled to live according to this perspective by sharing in the freedom of

Jesus from himself and his freedom to be for others; the Easter experience is precisely the way in which the freedom of Jesus became 'contagious'.

This is on a par with the contention of the British philosopher R. B. Braithwaite, that when someone says 'I believe in God the Father Almighty' he really means 'I intend to treat all men as my brothers'. This view did not gain wide Christian acceptance. *The Secular City* was perhaps nearer the concerns of the ordinary intelligent Christian. After a somewhat forced interpretation of the Old Testament as being concerned with human social activity rather than God's actions on behalf of man (the Sinai covenant being 'the desacralizing of values'), Harvey Cox salutes Jesus as the giver of freedom to all men in every situation, and as the personification of the Kingdom of God. This Kingdom is in process of realizing itself, and the Church is God's *avant-garde* in continuing and completing that process, which is the work of both God and man. This message he applies in particular to the needs and possibilities of the modern city; Jesus is the exorcist of the demonic powers which infest its life and the healer of the 'urban factions' which prevent its progress. And the Church, in its capacity of *diakonos*, servant, of the city, is God's agent. But if it is to perform its task it must be a community which, if not fully liberated, is in the process of liberation from 'compulsive patterns of behaviour based on mistaken images of the world'. And where does God meet us as we fulfil our Christian task? 'At those places in life where we come up against what is not pliable and disposable, at those hard edges where we are both stopped and challenged to move ahead. He meets us as the transcendent, at those aspects of our experience which can never be transmuted into extensions of ourselves.' And if we discover that the old names of God will not do, and a new one has to be found to signify the ways in which he acts in our time, there is nothing to be afraid of in that.

Without doubt there is an atheistic strain in the thought of some of these of whom an account has just been given, and other parts which can be misinterpreted as atheism. It was left to two other American theologians, T. J. J. Altizer of Emory

University, Georgia, and W. Hamilton, to develop these elements in the thinking of the 'secular theologians' and come up with what they called Christian Atheism. Altizer wrote a book called *The Gospel of Christian Atheism*, which had a short vogue in England, as in America. In this he contends that God died when Jesus came, there being, presumably, no further need for him. Altizer does not clearly indicate whether it is God himself who proved to be mortal, or our concept of God. But the phrase 'the death of God' was much publicized until the phrase 'Christian Atheism' was at last widely seen to be a contradiction in terms.

The end-product in Britain and America of this unconventional thinking of the early and middle sixties was not negligible, though it did not amount to the 'new Reformation' for which John Robinson hoped. It produced a group of 'radical theologians' in every denomination who claimed to strip the Gospel down to its essentials, had little use for the structures or doctrinal formulations of the Churches and despised metaphysical thinking, but had an immense respect for the historical Jesus and identified themselves wholeheartedly with the poor of the world. The parable of the Sheep and the Goats was their theme song, for to serve the deprived was identical with serving Christ. They certainly vindicated and proclaimed in theory and practice the secularity (in the Van Buren-Harvey Cox sense) of the Gospel. Whether they made many new converts to Christianity is doubtful, but they certainly widened the social understanding of Christian people, and retained within the Church many who would otherwise have left it.*

At first sight 'secular', 'radical' theology has little to do with the progress of ecumenism, and it is true that those who embraced it were only rarely engaged in the intricate matter of church union negotiations, and some of them were not indisposed to cast ridicule on the whole notion of uniting the useless structures of outdated institutions. But, almost *malgré lui*, this theology did in fact make a positive contribution to ecumenical thinking by questioning the old denominational dogmatisms and rigid structures. It helped to create an

© *New Christian* was their vigorous but rather short-lived periodical.

atmosphere in which every traditional belief and practice could be at least discussed, and the problems which were common to all the Churches brought to light. It also broadened the doctrine of salvation to include the material and corporate life of human beings as well as their souls, and so prepared the way for the so-called 'political theology' of the World Council at Uppsala and later. Moreover, it implicitly drew attention to the fact that in the face of the issues with which the Church and the world have to struggle in the present period denominational affiliations have very little relevance; in this struggle the whole Church must think and work in harmony, or its thought and work have very little effect on the life of the world. So it may be that the theological mood of the sixties, reflecting the whole mood of the times, though it shocked the orthodox, helped to pull the Churches out of the rut into which they had fallen.

A little of this, but perhaps not enough, was in the minds of the representatives, clerical and lay, from all the Churches who assembled at Nottingham for the Faith and Order Conference, called by the British Council of Churches, in September 1964. Christian unity was the main theme, and it certainly dominated the programme. It could be said, with some truth, that the occasion marked the coming-of-age of ecumenism in Britain. Those who came to Nottingham under the impact of pure idealism, or with the view that a beautiful unity of the Spirit was all that was required and could easily be achieved, were brought down to earth by discovering the sheer intractability of many denominational differences. Those who came in unconscious ignorance of what had already been achieved, or even suspicious that the 'high-ups' in the Churches were leading them into a bogus Paradise, were informed, brought up to date, and in most cases persuaded. From now on the quest for unity could be carried on realistically by those who knew both its promise and its difficulties.

The Conference issued two major challenges to the Churches. It called upon them all, first, in the regions in which they were situated (that is, in England, Wales, Scotland and Northern Ireland), 'to covenant together to work and pray for the inauguration of a union by a date agreed amongst them'.

And it expressed the hope 'that this date should not be later than Easter day, 1980'. Second, in pursuance of the 'Lund principle', 'to designate "areas of ecumenical experiment", at the request of local congregations, or in new towns and housing areas'. There was a much heavier vote for the call to a covenant than there was for the hope that Easter Day 1980 would be the date for the inauguration of union (for many thought that this hope tied the Holy Spirit down to a time-table); the vote for 'areas of ecumenical experiment' was unanimous. In the months and years that followed nearly all the Churches refused, for the time being at least, to commit themselves to the making of a covenant; but a slow and steady movement for setting up the 'areas' did begin shortly after and is still continuing.

The Nottingham Conference also urged 'that negotiations between particular churches already in hand be seen as steps towards this goal' (of unity). The Anglican-Methodist Conversations were clearly in mind, and their merits and prospects were vigorously argued by all those who were present.

Meanwhile these Conversations, started in 1955, had gone steadily on. An 'Interim Report' in 1958 had declared that the goal of intercommunion between the two Churches was not adequate, and should be replaced by that of organic union; it proceeded to make some preliminary suggestions as to how this could be reached. The two Churches accepted the Report, and officially made organic union their goal. The two teams therefore settled down to the arguments necessary to justify it. The progress of their work, the vicissitudes which followed and the final upshot provide object lessons in ecumenism which Church Union negotiators of the future will neglect at their peril.

In 1963 the teams published their definitive Report. It discussed the theological issues thought likely to be a matter of divergence between the Churches—Scripture and Tradition, Church Order, with special attention to Priesthood and Episcopacy, and the Sacraments. At every point the signatories stated that although there were differences of emphasis between the Churches on certain not unimportant matters, there was certainly enough agreement on doctrinal questions to justify and encourage the coming together of the two Churches into one. They went on to outline a procedure for this to happen in two stages. The first would be inaugurated by a service in which the ministers and members of the two Churches would be 'reconciled', and the two Churches would enter into full communion with each other; from the beginning of Stage I all new Methodist ministers would be ordained by a bishop in the historic succession according to an agreed Ordinal, and certain Methodist ministers would be consecrated as bishops; but the Churches would remain separate. After an interval, the length of which would be decided by the speed with which the two Churches grew together in understanding and purpose, Stage II, the stage of complete organic union, would be initiated.

Integral to the scheme was the form which the 'Service of Reconciliation' would take. It was proposed that there should be a solemn 'Declaration of Intention', in which it was to be stated that 'neither . . . wishes to call in question the reality and spiritual effectiveness of the ministry of the other Church', and that 'we wish to share each the spiritual heritage of the other . . . and to assure to our united Churches a ministry fully accredited in the eyes of all their members'. And then that the members of each Church, and the ministers of each Church, in that order, should be accepted by each other, the ministers (including the bishops of the Church of England) by the reciprocal laying on of hands.

But not all members of both teams signed the Report. All the Anglicans did, but four Methodists dissented, and issued their own statement. The leader of the four was Professor Kingsley Barrett of Durham, very eminent in New Testament scholarship. The dissentients expressed the view that the Report placed too much emphasis on Tradition and too little on Scripture; that historic episcopacy, depending, as it did, on the strictest invariability of ordination by bishops in succession from the apostles, was unacceptable to Methodists; and that the whole scheme placed in jeopardy the Methodist doctrine of the Priesthood of all Believers.

Debates followed in both Churches, but they do not appear

at this point to have reached the ordinary members in large numbers, except in some parts of the country. Methodist opponents of the scheme formed an organisation illegitimately and inaccurately known as the 'Voice of Methodism'; but the four 'Dissentients', whose objections were more theological than those of the 'Voice', did not join. By 1965 the time had come for a decision on whether the Report offered the right way forward. The Convocations of the Church of England and the Methodist Conference both decided by large majorities that it did, and appointed two further teams, including several from the old ones, but also several new members, to deal with some objections, clarify some outstanding issues, compose an Ordinal which could be approved for use in Stage I, and present a fully articulated scheme in all necessary detail. Harold Roberts remained Chairman of the Methodist group, the Bishop of London, Robert Stopford, became Anglican Chairman. The Roman Catholic Church in England, and the English Free Churches, were invited to send observers to various sessions of the Commission.

The going was harder for the new teams than they had expected, for it soon appeared that much opposition which had remained latent so far was coming out into the open and marshalling its arguments and supporters. Each objection old and new was carefully scrutinized and faithfully dealt with by the Commission; but a chill descended on the conversationalists twice during their deliberations, for the first time when it was announced that the Church of England was to require a 75 per cent majority in the Convocations for the scheme to be approved (it was well-known that this was a very difficult objective to achieve in Convocation on any major issue)*; for the second time when it was announced that a referendum would be held among all the beneficed clergymen of the Church of England (a great number of whom, in rural areas, had virtually no knowledge of Methodism).

Nevertheless the Commission as a whole developed a profound unity of purpose and understanding which kept alive the vision that motivated all its members. The eventual Report was approved unanimously by the whole Commission, except

* The Methodist Conference felt bound to adopt a similar procedure.

for Dr James Packer, a leading Evangelical Anglican, who could not accept a Service of Reconciliation that could be construed as ordination. Another Anglican, who had signed the Report, changed his mind later on.

The Commission composed, with the help of other liturgists from outside its ranks, an Ordinal which gained universal acclaim, and gave it a Preface which was equally approved. It also refined and refined again the Service of Reconciliation until it left no doubt that in the laying of hands on each minister of both Churches in turn the Holy Spirit was being asked to grant to each minister what he needed for the fulfilment of the larger ministry that was now to be his. In this way it was left open to anyone who so desired to regard the laying on of hands as an act of ordination. But this was by no means the necessary or implied meaning. The word 'presbyter' or 'elder', which is used of the Christian ministry in the New Testament, whereas 'priest' is not (it came into use two centuries later), was proposed for future use instead of either 'priest' or 'minister', as a reconciling word.

In addition, the Commission's Report re-stated the conviction that there was sufficient agreement in doctrine for the Churches to go forward; argued the case for a two-stage, rather than a one-stage, scheme; discussed the role of Methodist bishops in the light of new concepts of episcopacy; assured the Methodist Church that it would not be expected to break its relations with other Free Churches; made practical suggestions for the growing together of the Churches in Stage One; and went into the matters of Lay Ministries, the Diaconate, Christian Initiation and the relations of Church and State.

Having discharged its work, the Commission and the Churches eagerly awaited the results. The matter was discussed in both Churches at every level, perhaps more widely (though this is hard to tell) in the Methodist Church than in the Church of England, and very often at joint meetings with speakers from both Churches. There is little doubt that a sizeable majority in both Churches came to support strongly the acceptance of the Scheme.

But opposition was launched in full force. The Voice of

Methodism persuaded groups of Methodists in certain parts of the country, notably the North West, that the Scheme endangered the very heart of Methodist witness, and that historic episcopacy was intolerable. But when it came to the voting in the Circuits and the Districts, while the mandate at the Circuit level was not everywhere wholehearted, every District Synod voted for the Scheme, sometimes by overwhelming majorities. The only substantial success of the Voice of Methodism was in persuading many Anglicans that it was more influential than it actually was.

Anglican objections were more variegated. Geoffrey Fisher had retired from the archiepiscopate of Canterbury in 1961; nevertheless he bombarded his successor, Michael Ramsey, members of the Commission, and many other people, with ceaseless reiterations of his view that his original notion of intercommunion, without organic union to follow, was all that was required. He no doubt exercised some influence on those who had admired his initiative in the past.

The Anglo-Catholics were divided; some regarded the Scheme as the best, perhaps the only way of preserving the Catholic order of the Church of England and uniting at the same time with a Free Church; others held that all Methodist ministers, not being already ordained, must be episcopally ordained before their orders could be recognized by the Church of England, and that the Service of Reconciliation did not effect this.

The solidest bloc of opposition was formed by the Evangelicals, who objected to the Service of Reconciliation on exactly opposite grounds to those of the Anglo-Catholics. Methodist ministers, to them, were already ordained, and simple recognition was all that was needed for full communion to be established. They saw the Service of Reconciliation as, in fact, an ordination, and said that it must be rejected for this reason.

In the minds of many people who were not committed either to support or to opposition there lingered, it must be acknowledged, a certain distaste for the 'ambiguity' of the Service of Reconciliation. Surely it could be stated outright whether it was intended to confer ordination or not? It may be that the reasons for not doing this, and for the ambiguity that resulted, were not made clear enough, nor was it pointed out with sufficient force that ambiguity is indeed culpable when it is covertly employed to paper over or conceal a difference of conviction, but perfectly honourable when it is openly accepted in order to recognize a difference of conviction and transcend it.

Against the various objections, and the further unjustified assertion that union with the Methodists would make union with the Church of Rome impossibly remote, the Archbishops of Canterbury and York, with the great majority of the other bishops and of the large body of central Anglicans, stood firm in the conviction that the Scheme offered a Biblical means of healing a grievous wound in the Body of Christ. The referendum of the beneficed clergy was in favour of the Scheme, though not conclusively so. The great majority of the dioceses voted for the Scheme with large, moderate or small majorities.

It was arranged that the decisive debates in the two Churches should take place simultaneously in Birmingham and London in early July 1969. The Methodist Conference, despite a powerful speech in opposition by Professor Kingsley Barrett, approved the Scheme by a majority well above the 75 per cent which it had been agreed that both Churches needed to have. Then the Conference hoped and feared till the news from London arrived. When it came, it was that the Anglican vote in favour was under 70 per cent. The Evangelicals and the Anglo-Catholics, despite their very different views, had voted together, and an uncalculated number of others had supported them in order to avoid a split in the Church of England.

The supporters of the Scheme in both Churches made one more effort three years later. A joint committee, set up by the Archbishop of Canterbury and the President of the Methodist Conference, had agreed that the Service of Reconciliation could be understood, by those who wished to do so, as a 'conditional ordination'. But this failed to satisfy the Anglo-Catholic opponents, and the pattern of 1969 was repeated, despite a most moving speech by Archbishop Ramsey, with a slightly reduced Anglican majority.

UNCERTAIN BRITAIN IN THE SIXTIES

Historians, looking back on these events from a greater distance than can at present be compassed, may well conclude that the failure of the Scheme was primarily due to the ingrained fear of basic change which is not uncommon among Christians. Certainly the theological arguments were not strong enough in themselves to defeat the Scheme, and in any case mostly cancelled each other out.

However this may be, a golden opportunity was lost. Whether this was an unmitigated disaster, or a disaster mitigated by the lessons learned from it for the future, remains uncertain. We may certainly take comfort from the fact that since the 'breakdown' both the Church of England and the Methodist Church have advanced towards a truer appreciation of each other's ministries and a less rigid use of the old categories of 'validity' and 'succession' which have proved so divisive in the past. And it may be that the other English Free Churches, which had been reluctant to join in union negotiations a few years earlier, and were in any case dubious about some aspects of the Scheme, now felt that a new start would soon be possible in which they could wholeheartedly share. Those who suffered grievously from the defeat of the Scheme will rejoice if a new and better, perhaps more flexible, scheme rises, phoenix-like, from the ashes of the old.

CHAPTER EIGHT

Hope Awaiting Fulfilment

THE THESIS has been sturdily maintained by many people that success in bringing together the Church of England and the Methodist Church would have provided a powerful fillip to similar types of Church union all over the British Commonwealth, and that the failure of the Anglican-Methodist Scheme correspondingly impeded them. Certainly union schemes for Sri Lanka, Nigeria and Ghana have subsequently faltered, though only the Nigerian Scheme is quite dead, and the only schemes which have succeeded, such as that for the Uniting Church of Australia (1977), lack Anglican participation. But a causal connection is hard to establish, and in each case of failure, or possible failure, many local non-religious factors have entered the situation, not least Methodist internal dissensions.

The Anglican-Methodist breakdown could not in any case prevent the consummation of union in Pakistan and North India, which took place in November 1970. Here in both cases the Christian constituency was much smaller than in South India, and it had long seemed absurd for it to be divided into several denominations in face of the overwhelming majority of Hindus, Muslims and animists.

The uniting Churches were the Anglican Church of India, Pakistan and Ceylon, the United Church of North India (Congregationalist–Presbyterian), the Methodist Church derived from the British Methodists, a number of Baptist congregations, the Church of the Brethren and the Disciples of Christ. Until a date very near that of union the United Methodist Church (derived from American Methodism) the largest non-Roman Church in the whole of North India, participated, but then it withdrew. The reasons alleged reflected little credit on any Church, but were difficult to disentangle; they certainly included a considerable disparity between the material wealth of the United Methodist Church (which was considerable) and that of the others (which was small).

The principles of union adopted, and the procedure followed in the Service of Inauguration, with the reciprocal laying on of hands, were closely similar to those laid down in the Anglican-Methodist Scheme, except that union took place in one stage, not two. The Church of England, though it could not bring itself to accept such a Scheme for England, had approved it for North India. Yet the local and personal difficulties encountered on the way to union prompted the preacher at the Service of Inauguration to preach on the text: 'A woman in labour is in pain because her time has come; but when the child is born she forgets the anguish in her joy that a man has been born into the world' (John 16:21). Certainly the joy in the vast marquee in Nagpur which contained the congregation of 6,000 was immense, and the heavy tasks facing the Christian Church in a country of intractable social and economic problems have been bravely faced.

Nearer home, Scotland was scarcely affected by the Anglican-Methodist decisions, and multilateral conversations aimed at uniting all the non-Roman Catholic Churches were continuing in an unspectacular way. A positive attempt began in 1972 to unite the Methodist District of Scotland with the Church of Scotland, and proposals to this effect appeared in 1977. But the Methodist District turned them down in 1978, in fear of being absorbed by a much larger Church. In Wales, too, nearly all the denominations pressed forward to a Covenant for Unity in the spirit of Nottingham, 1964. Yet although they have covenanted to unite, the traditional problems of the ministry have so far held up actual union.

In England the mood of the Church of England and Methodism was distinctly chastened. Very many Methodists and Anglicans were sadly disappointed, and many ecumenical Anglicans were unwilling for a time to begin new discussions for fear of another failure. But the two Churches were saved from sinking into complete lethargy by the urgency of many practical problems, notably the financial situation, which was slowly deteriorating, and the decline in the number of candidates for ordination (corresponding roughly, in proportion, to the decline in communicant membership). Liturgical and administrative reform were also urgent issues. The tendency now, of course, was to deal with such problems denominationally, and it was on denominational lines that both Churches 're-structured' their organization, their activities and their liturgies. The introduction of synodical government in the Church of England had, in any case, long been planned, and came into operation in 1970, while the Anglican-Methodist Scheme still had a possibility of success; it was the logical consequence of the Life and Liberty Movement of fifty years before, and meant that at all levels of Church government the laity had a say in decision-making which had previously been denied to it. This was gradually worked out in practice during the following years. Methodist re-structuring was aimed at simplifying the labyrinth of committee work to which Methodism is prone, and at providing the President of the Conference (who holds office only for a year) with a Council to advise both him and the Conference. The new Methodist Church Act of 1976, carried through the Church and Parliament in the face of determined opposition by a small minority, removed the power over property wielded by local trustees, and made it possible, under severe restriction, for the 'doctrinal clauses' of the Methodist Constitution to be amended by the Conference.

The Church of England Liturgical Commission produced a further rite of Holy Communion (Series III, following on Series II of a few years earlier), an Ordinal and other Services, and advanced towards the production of a new Prayer Book. The Methodist Faith and Order Committee, going forward on similar lines, completed twelve years' work, including the writing of 'The Sunday Service' (the communion rite) and a new Ordinal, by successfully recommending to the Conference of 1975 the publication of the *Methodist Service Book*. A supplement to the Methodist Hymn Book, containing a number of contemporary songs and melodies, had been published in 1969, under the title of *Hymns and Songs*.

Perhaps the most lamentable result of the Anglican-

HOPE AWAITING FULFILMENT

Methodist breakdown was the failure to press on with joint theological training (which was plainly required by economics, ecumenics and educational principle). The Queen's College, Birmingham, was formed in 1970 by the union of the Anglican Queen's College and the Methodist Handsworth College (with places for members of other denominations), and its success has drawn necessary attention to the absence of similar ventures elsewhere in Britain. At the time of Anglican-Methodist decision schemes for bringing together other colleges of the two denominations were in the minds of many, but these never came to full fruition, and each of the two Churches grappled alone with the painful necessity of choosing which colleges to close. Ecumenical collaboration has, however, been set up in Cambridge and Manchester.

An important event which was of necessity denominational, and had clear ecumenical implications, was the decision of the Methodist Conference to ordain women. The matter had been under discussion in the Church for more than three decades, and the Conference had long ago ruled that there was no theological objection. The mind of the Church was steadily made up during the fifties and sixties that the time had come to proceed to action. But those who favoured this most strongly were frequently those who most strongly supported the Anglican-Methodist Scheme, and they carefully refrained from pressing the matter while this was awaiting decision, though it was well known that in due course the matter would be pressed. After the decisions of the Church of England, there was no longer any occasion for delay. An overwhelming vote was registered in 1970 for the ordination of women on the same terms as men, apart from liberty to interrupt active ministry for a time when necessary, and the first women were ordained in 1974. This event caused none of the disturbances that were predicted by critics, and women ministers rapidly became wholly accepted members of the Methodist ministry, as they already were in the other English Free Churches.

This issue is still undecided in the Church of England, though here also it has now been officially recognized that there are no theological objections. Among the arguments

111

put forward against the ordination of women, is the one that since Jesus was a man and not a woman, his High Priesthood can be continued in the Church on earth only by those of the same sex as he, and it is pointed out that all the apostles were men. Others find it hard to believe that every woman is denied a call to the ordained ministry simply on the ground of her sex, and point out that the selection of women as apostles was impossible in the social conditions of the time. Ecumenically, it needs to be stated that the majority of Churches in the world, including several in the Anglican communion, ordain women or are about to do so, while the majority of Christians belong to the two great Communions that are set against it—the Roman Catholic and the Orthodox. The ecumenical balance is nicely poised; the Church of England is finding it hard to make up its mind, as it must surely wish to do, on the merits of the case in the light of its own faith and life, as well as of the total ecumenical situation. It is subject to strong pressures from without and within to hold its hand in the matter, while, paradoxically enough, there is a growing campaign in the Roman Catholic Church to ordain women.

During the early seventies the British Council of Churches, now passing into the fourth decade of its existence, continued to provide a useful forum for the exchange of ideas between Church leaders. It did not, however, play the leading role which some expected of it in the resumption of ecumenical activity at a time when it was often said that the 'steam' had gone out of the Ecumenical Movement. But the strength of such a Council as this depends entirely on the (not simply financial) support which it receives from its member-Churches. It did call a conference of Church leaders in Birmingham in 1973 to consider the Churches' programme for the future, and signs of more vigorous life appeared when Harry Morton, the new General Secretary, initiated a careful, nation-wide appraisal of British society. The results of this are set out in *Britain Today and Tommorrow*, and this new approach may lead to a well-thought out and prepared-for 'Mission to the Nation'. Though the impact of the Council on the Churches and the nation, so far, has not been remarkable, the reports of its Working Parties over the years have often been illuminating—on sex, religious education in Secondary Schools, and various international problems, especially those of Southern Africa; and the Council has set up a permanent 'unit' on community relations in Britain.

But the main thrust towards unity has been outside the Council, though the Council has provided useful facilities. Primacy of honour must be given to the Presbyterian Church of England and the Congregational Church (formerly the Congregational Union), who came together to form the United Reformed Church in 1972. The union did not involve any great theological issues, for both Churches were in the 'Reformed' tradition which stems from John Calvin (without embracing his doctrine of predestination), and, in particular, the vexed questions of ministry and sacraments which hold up larger unions did not arise. But legal questions were complicated, old habits were challenged; and each party had to yield certain cherished positions on Church Order, the chief one of which was the traditional view of Congregationalists, still held by many, that each congregation is wholly autonomous under Christ.

The Church of England and the Methodist Church did not entirely lose touch with each other after the Anglican-Methodist votes. A Joint Liaison Commission was set up to prevent this from happening. The growing number, now running into several hundred, of 'Areas of Ecumenical Experiment' begun as a result of Nottingham 1964, was brought forcibly to its notice, and it successfully recommended to all the main Churches that they should set up a 'Consultative Council for Local Ecumenical Projects in England'.* C.C.L.E.P.E. has since then kept a watchful but helpful eye on much local activity.

The most striking and effective form of this activity is certainly to be found in the Areas of Ecumenical Experiment, spread unevenly over the country, but numerous in the dioceses of Bristol and Birmingham. In these 'A.E.E.s'—whether they be in new housing areas, settled suburbs, or villages—the congregations and ministers do as much together as denominational requirements allow, and engage

* The term 'Local Ecumenical Project' covers a wide range of activity.

in such experiments in worship and mission and ministry as they can persuade their denominational authorities to permit. Sometimes, it is to be feared, they do not use their liberty to the full; but often they become really and truly one congregation, one 'ecumenical parish' (as many like to call themselves), in which all the ministers are accepted as ministers of all, and all members are welcomed to the eucharists of all.

Many of these are Anglican and Methodist only; many include other denominations; the local Roman Catholic Church is often a friendly but partial participant. Often church buildings are legally shared according to the provisions of the Sharing of Church Buildings Act 1969—a rather cumbrous piece of legislation, the operation of which involves local congregations in great expense. All A.E.E.s have a 'Sponsoring Body'—appointed by the authorities of the Churches from clergy, ministers and laity to help and guide them. Sometimes a Sponsoring Body sponsors just one Area, sometimes all within a diocese.

It was from such an Area in Bristol that the notion of Joint Confirmation arose. The Bristol Sponsoring Body took up the idea, and now the Church authorities have agreed to a form of service (to be used where the local Church authorities agree) in which all the participating ministers lay hands on all the confirmands and all the confirmands become full members of all the participating Churches.

It can well be that these local enterprises will in the end be found to have done more to promote the union of Christians than the most carefully worked-out schemes of ecclesiastical union. For they involve individual Christians and groups of Christians, personally and every day, in ecumenical life, and so form the solid foundation on which Christian unity can be built. And it is not to be forgotten that here, at the 'grass roots' (a phrase badly overused in this connexion), Roman Catholics, in spite of official limitations, are being steadily integrated into the communal life of other Christians. Schemes of union and local ecumenism are two necessary parts, no doubt, of the one whole.

The fact that the House of Bishops in 1976 sanctioned the use of the Joint Confirmation Service when the diocesan

HOPE AWAITING FULFILMENT

bishop agreed indicated that changes of attitude were taking place in the Church of England. This was also shown by the General Synod's passing in 1972 of Canon B15A, which admits to Holy Communion in Anglican Churches all members of the mainstream Churches 'in good standing', though it requires the incumbent ultimately to ask a regular communicant from a Free Church to consider whether he or she should be episcopally confirmed. This measure was taken by some enthusiasts to show that full intercommunion had arrived, but in fact this is not so, though it means that Free Church people can come freely to Anglican eucharists as welcome guests.

These developments—and others could be added, such as the formation of about two hundred, mostly small, Methodist–U.R.C. Churches—were undoubtedly refreshing. Yet British ecumenism in the seventies certainly needed the injection of new ideas and new energy from the World Church. The Faith and Order Commission of the World Council of Churches began to supply this, for those who were willing to receive it, at its meeting in Louvain, Belgium, in 1971, when it widened the scope of the ecumenical idea by taking as its theme 'The Unity of the Church and the Unity of Mankind'. The theme itself was treated in a way that seemed to many to be over-academic, but it was now firmly on the ecumenical agenda; the unity of the Church is seen not as an end in itself, but as a stage in and a means towards the unity of all mankind and above all as a 'sign' of what is to come. Louvain also welcomed and took for granted the participation of Roman Catholic theologians—and the meeting was held in a Roman Catholic Seminary. Furthermore it began, as a necessary consequence of the Uppsala Assembly of the W.C.C., to look at theological questions not in the abstract but as they present themselves in the actual situations of our times. It was in this context that the Sacraments, the Ministry, Unity, and the authority of the Bible were studied; and it was in this context that the hope of a genuinely universal Council of the whole Church in the whole world, first mentioned at Uppsala, was repeated and emphasized.

The Louvain processes of thought were carried considerably

115

further at the next meeting of the Faith and Order Commission in 1974, in Accra, Ghana. This was the first meeting of the Commission to be held in the Third World, and it proved to be the most exhilarating ecumenical experience that the members of the Commission, many of them conference-and case-hardened veterans, had ever had. The warm hospitality of the Ghanaians, the exuberance of a new nation in a developing continent, the drums and dances of African Christian worship—all of them penetrated into the heart of the theological discussion, and all of them contributed to the diverse unity of the whole occasion.

But Ghana was also a centre of the serious economic problems which face the Third World, and will continue to do so until the First World realizes and fulfils its responsibilities; and because the meeting was in Africa there was a larger number of black theologians, many of whom were black politicians also, than ever before, and they were certainly prepared to reiterate constantly the causes for African and Asian anger and suspicion against the affluent Western world.

The main theme was Hope—the neglected third member of the Pauline triad. Hope was interpreted theologically, of course, as grounded in the saving activity of God for all mankind; but it was not thought of as hope simply for the world to come, but also and at the same time (and here the leadership of Jürgen Moltmann, the German theologian of hope, was especially evident) as hope for this world, hope of a just human society in which all will be free to develop their gifts, and those now oppressed—on grounds of race or class or sex or religion—will shed their handicaps and restraints. And when it was asked: what is hope? the answer came in a litany prepared for the use of the Commission:

'Hope is a mother awaiting the birth of her child:
    a band of Blacks singing: "We are climbing Jacob's ladder";
    a young woman on her wedding day;
    a little child looking forward to Christmas;
    a fanfare of drums announcing an African eucharist;
    an oppressed person returning good for evil;

a choir of lepers singing the Hallelujah chorus;
Jesus praying for his enemies.'

In this setting up of a quest for unity in hope, new statements on the Ministry, Baptism and the Eucharist were formulated. These have been 'sent down' to the Churches world-wide. Their active participation in the discussion is invited, in the expectation that out of numerous consultations and varied experiences a consensus will gradually emerge which will finally put an end to the misunderstandings of the past and create a new theological harmony for the future. In furthering such a consensus the Faith and Order Department of the W.C.C. has a significant role to fulfil, and in Britain the British Council of Churches is playing its part.

The concept of 'Conciliarity', first discussed at Louvain, was worked out further at Accra; according to this a stage in the coming of union, or indeed in some cases the coming of union itself, might be the assembling of councils, representing all the Churches involved, not only at national and international level, but also at local and regional level.

And something else emerged, almost unnoticeably, at Accra. The traditional concept of unity was of unity between Churches and Christians. Is not the community of black and white, of women and men, of ex-oppressor and ex-oppressed, in the same Church, also a vital part of the unity of Christian people?

The Fifth Assembly of the World Council of Churches met in Nairobi, Kenya, in 1975. It was not a turning point in the history of the Ecumenical Movement in the way in which the Uppsala Assembly was, but it corrected some of the imbalance detected by some at Uppsala, while confirming the general direction which the World Council was taking. Many participants at Nairobi held that Uppsala had emphasized political salvation for oppressed peoples at the expense of spiritual evangelism, and Nairobi was keen to show that the two belong together. The World Council, from the time of Uppsala, had been charged with harping on the injustice and oppression of which white governments in Southern Africa were guilty, and forgetting the oppressions perpetrated in Eastern Europe. It had to be pointed out that the invaluable presence at ecumenical conferences of delegations from the U.S.S.R. and other countries of Eastern Europe laid upon the World Council the duty of not endangering their life or liberty on their return to their own countries; but the Council found a way of protesting as firmly against the oppression of whites by whites and blacks, as against that of blacks by whites and blacks. The influence of the Churches of the Third World on those of the rest of the world was exemplified and tempered by Philip Potter, himself a black West Indian, now General Secretary of the W.C.C.

The British Press gave much more coverage to the Nairobi Assembly than it had to Uppsala, perhaps having belatedly realized that the World Council was an important factor in world affairs. Although some of the newspapers still gave the impression that the Programme to Combat Racism was almost the sole concern of the Council (actually it is one of several hundred concerns), the British churchgoer did thus become better informed on ecumenical matters. Yet there was something much nearer home to which English Christians ought also to have been giving their attention in preparation for decisions which would soon affect them. In 1972 the Church Leaders' Conference in Birmingham discussed again, of course, the question of Church Unity, but action was not yet possible. In January 1973 an informal conference of leaders from all the English Churches met at Christ Church, Oxford, after some preliminary conversations among some of them. From the Christ Church conference emerged a plan to hold 'Talks about Talks', and it was highly proper that the recently formed United Reformed Church should take the initiative in inviting all the Churches to engage in these. From the 'Talks about Talks' came the 'Churches' Unity Commission', officially appointed by the Baptist Union, the Churches of Christ, the Congregational Federation (formed of the Congregational Churches that did not join the United Reformed Church), the Moravian Church, the Methodist Church, the Roman Catholic Church), the United Reformed Church and the Church of England. John Huxtable, who had done much to bring about the formation of the U.R.C., became the Excutive Officer, Patrick Rodger, Bishop of

Manchester, the Chairman, and Kenneth Greet, Secretary of the Methodist Conference, the Vice-Chairman.

After a period of quiet brooding, the Commission issued, in January 1976, 'Ten Propositions'. These were, in effect, a summons to all the Churches in England to promote visible (this term was preferred to 'organic') unity by entering a covenant (a) to recognize each others' members as 'true members of the Body of Christ and to welcome them to Holy Communion without conditions'; (b) to recognize each others' ministries as 'true ministries of word and sacraments in the Holy Catholic Church'; (c) to agree on mutually acceptable rites of initiation (i.e. baptism and confirmation) to be used in all the Covenanting Churches; (d) to take the historic episcopacy into the system of the non-episcopal Churches; (e) to explore further steps to make more clearly visible the unity of all Christ's people. The Propositions also included provisions for ensuring that Churches which could not make the Covenant remained in 'close fellowship and consultation' with those which did.

The discussion of the Propositions within the Churches came only slowly into operation, although the Commission asked in the first place for definitive decisions by 1977; so the year of decision was altered to 1978 (a much more reasonable date, in any case, for the Church of England, because of the complexity of its organization). Gradually the discussion spread over all the Churches, but did not generate either the opposition that had been feared or the enthusiasm that had been hoped for.

The bishops of the Roman Catholic Church in England replied, in due course, that they could not enter the Covenant, since the clauses which covered the recognition of members and ministers did not accord with Roman Catholic doctrine. They expressed the hope, however, that the other Churches *would* make the Covenant. The Congregational Federation rejected the Propositions out of hand; it objected to episcopacy. The Baptist Union (not a Church, of course, but a 'union' of independent congregations) reluctantly agreed not to recommend the Covenant to its constituents, though individual congregations were free to join in. The Churches of

119

Christ and the Moravian Church agreed to enter the Covenant. The United Reformed Church took the same decision, but expressed the wish that certain questions about the individual episcopate should be further discussed. The Methodist Church agreed to enter the Covenant as soon as the Church of England was willing to do so—and went on to explain that if it ever turned out to be right for the Free Churches to unite with each other without the participation of the Church of England, a covenant would not be necessary, since they already recognised each others' ministries and members.

This put the ball squarely and (surely) fairly in the court of the Church of England. During the year 1977–8 the dioceses had been asked to debate and vote on the resolution that the Ten Propositions afforded a good basis for further consultation. The dioceses, with few exceptions, showed a desire to move towards unity in the way indicated by the Propositions, without committing themselves yet to all the Propositions as such, and the official resolutions put before the General Synod were therefore stronger than the somewhat feeble one submitted to the dioceses. The chief were: (i) The Church of England affirms its readiness to proceed by discussion towards covenanting on the basis of the Ten Propositions with all those Churches which are so willing. (ii) Such discussions in no way prejudge the admissibility and acceptability of women to the ordained ministry of the Church of England. (iii) The Church of England engages in these discussions on the further understanding that a form of covenant will be drafted by the parties concerned within the next two years. This will incorporate agreements that will already have been reached with each Church on the questions raised on both sides in reply to the Ten Propositions. The Church of England will then be able to decide whether or not to enter into that specific covenant.

Those resolutions were approved by an overall majority of approximately 80 per cent. An additional resolution, altered by amendment and passed by the same majority, stipulated that the covenant should include 'incorporating the existing ministries into the historic threefold ministry by invocation of the Spirit in a prayer which makes clear that such incorporation is intended and conveyed, by a distinctive sign for the conferring of a gift of the Spirit, and by concelebration of Holy Communion'.

The implications of the additional resolution need careful discussion during the period of the drawing up of the covenant, since a new element has now been introduced. What is the 'distinctive sign for the conferring of a gift of the Holy Spirit' to be? It can scarcely be the laying-on-of-hands. This would seem to some to be a covert introduction of ordination; to others it would be unpleasantly ambiguous (and it was this 'ambiguity' that helped to bring down the Anglican-Methodist Scheme). And it must not in any sense diminish the impact of the 'recognition' of existing ministries. Free Church opinion would not sanction that; and Anglican opinion, as reflected in a 1977 conference at High Leigh, held in order 'to seek a view representative of the widest possible constituency within the Church of England', would be equally against it. The Church of England in general has certainly moved a long way in its attitude to Free Church ministries since the Anglican-Methodist Scheme.

Perhaps the ancient rite of the Kiss of Peace, which signifies repentance, free acceptance of each other and the harmony based on reconciliation, would suit the case, so long as it included a prayer to the Holy Spirit to confer the incorporation of each Church's ministry into the ministry of the others—and thus of non-episcopal ministries into the historic threefold ministry.

Thus the covenant and the covenanting service will need great patience in the drawing up. Anglican emphasis on the value of the historic episcopate and the ministries derived from it, Free Church emphasis on the value of the presbyterate, which is held to be derived from the New Testament, full and free mutual recognition (including, of course, the recognition of the women ministers of the Methodist and United Reformed Churches), invocation of the Holy Spirit to bestow the needed gifts of ministry on all concerned and to bring true reconciliation between the ministries and people of the covenanting Churches, the resolve to work out in the future new forms of episcopacy* and a new understanding of the place of the laity in all the Churches—all these must find a place.

Thus the crisis of ecumenism, long foreseen and expected, is now upon the Churches in England. They stand poised for a definitive decision about their whole future in the year 1980—which was the year that the Nottingham Conference of 1964 proposed for the sealing of the covenant of unity.

---

* It is perhaps noteworthy that the Methodist Conference in 1978 instituted an enquiry into the question whether the Methodist Church should take the step of 'including an episcopal form of ministry in its life' if delay in the progress towards unity was caused by other Churches' responses to the Ten Propositions.

EPILOGUE

The intertwined events in the life of the World Church which this book has tried to disentangle and describe by putting them into the categories of 'world-wide', 'World Council' and 'British' have shown clearly that the signing of the Covenant will not discharge the ecumenical task, even for England. It is one important step towards the organic unity, which is both inward and outward, institutional and spiritual, of Christ's people in this country. The history of the years so far shows clearly to each and all concerned the truth of the saying quoted in the Anglican-Methodist Report of 1963: 'It is not given to thee to finish the task, but neither art thou free to desist therefrom.'

But it also shows that if progress is to continue, the Churches and their leaders and their members will need to remember some quite elementary things often forgotten, and act in accordance with them.

(i) There must be no abatement of respect for each other's traditions. Respect does not mean saying (or merely thinking), 'they will do better when they learn better—from us'. This is patronizing tolerance. Respect means the willingness to enter imaginatively and appreciatively into the ways of worship, the spirituality, the ethical values, and even the constitutional procedures of other Churches, for all these are rooted in a particular experience of the divine grace. All of them, like our own (as all of us must say), are imperfect. We share them with each other for the sake of mutual enrichment.

(ii) When Churches engage in conversations with each other with a view to closer unity, they do so as equal partners, and must treat each other as such, even when one party is weaker in numbers and resources than the other, and perhaps especially then. No Church may settle, or interfere with, the affairs of another, nor claim to know what is best for it; but each Church is involved in the hopes and difficulties of every other Church within the Body of Christ, for we are all 'members of one another'. To forget them, or to remember those of some Churches and forget those of others, is to reject the ecumenical idea and postpone its realization.

(iii) The cause of continued divisions is as often social, historical, economic or political as it is theological. Most often of all, it is reluctance to change what has been valuable in the past, for fear of losing the psychological security which established ways of doing things provide. What seems to oneself to be a proper reverence for the past is seen by others as obstinacy or prejudice, and this is sometimes exactly what it is.

(iv) There is a special danger which besets the Ecumenical Movement in countries where one Church is considerably more powerful than the others—whether because of legal establishment or as the result of political or religious history; and it is a danger which is to be found not least in England and Scotland. The 'established' Church tends to assume, almost unthinkingly, that it has a natural right to take the lead and control the situation. The other Churches tend to assume, also unthinkingly, that they have a natural duty to vindicate their identity by opposition and self-assertion. This can bedevil relationships at many levels and impede progress even among those committed to unity.

(v) Christian truth is not totally possessed by any one Church, and not the least achievement of Vatican II was to acknowledge this. Differences in doctrine are as likely to cross denominational boundaries as to follow them. Therefore the consideration of Christian theology is a common task, not a denominational one. For instance, if it is true that the *Myth of God Incarnate*, published in 1977, strikes at the root of essential Christian teaching, then this is the concern of all Christians thinking together.

(vi) Christian unity is not an end in itself; it is for the sake of the Church's mission to the world. The immediate aim of those who seek for it is the uniting of Christians; their further aim is the unity of mankind. The Churches are not called to

EPILOGUE

huddle together; they are called to open themselves to the world by offering an example of diversity in unity to a world which knows little of unity and too much of diversity.

(vii) No nation is sufficient to itself in its understanding of Christianity, any more than in anything else. The world-wide community of Christians, mostly through the World Council of Churches and the global fellowship of the Church of Rome, but also in other ways, is seeking and already beginning to find a common mind on many great issues. It is the height of folly and sin for the Churches in any country to proceed on their own way as if this were not happening.

(viii) Conferences, councils, negotiations, propositions and schemes are all necessary, and it is not high-minded but unrealistic, and sometimes arrogant, to despise them. But they are useless unless the Spirit of God has been allowed to implant in the minds and imaginations of those who take part in them the vision of the Holy Catholic Church made visibly one, not by human ingenuity, but by divine love and power, and possessing a holiness beyond human ability to conceive or create.

The Lord of the Church still reigns; he requires of his people not success, but faithfulness and love.

SUGGESTED FURTHER READING (in addition to books mentioned in the text)

For general reading:
F. A. Iremonger: *William Temple*, O.U.P., 1948.
S. C. Neill (ed.): *Twentieth Century Christianity*, Collins, 1961.
A. R. Vidler (ed.): *Soundings*, C.U.P., 1962.
R. E. Davies: *Methodism*, Pelican and Epworth, 1963 and 1976.
D. L. Edwards and R. E. Davies: *Unity begins at home* (report of the Nottingham Conference), S.C.M., 1964.
A. R. Vidler: *20th Century Defenders of the Faith*, S.C.M., 1965.
R. Lloyd: *The Church of England, 1900–1965*, S.C.M., 1966.
K. Slack: *Uppsala Report*, S.C.M., 1968.
D. L. Edwards: *Religion and Change*, Hodder and Stoughton, 1969.
B. Till: *The Churches Search for Unity*, Pelican, 1972.

For research:
G. K. A. Bell: *Documents on Christian Unity*, O.U.P., 1924–58.
R. Rouse and S. C. Neill: *History of the Ecumenical Movement, 1517–1948*, S.P.C.K., 1954 and 1967.
Anglican–Methodist Unity: Interim Report, 1958; *The Report*, 1963; *The Ordinal*, 1968; *The Scheme*, 1968, S.P.C.K. and Epworth.
World Council of Churches Faith and Order Documents: obtainable from the British Council of Churches, 10 Eaton Gate, London SW1.
Abbott and Gallagher: *Documents of Vatican II*, Chapman, 1966.

Modern Ecumenical Documents on the Eucharist, S.P.C.K., 1973.
Modern Ecumenical Documents on the Ministry, S.P.C.K., 1975.
Authority in the Church (Anglican-Roman Catholic International Commission), S.P.C.K., 1976.
Growth in Understanding (Methodist-Catholic), Epworth, 1977.

INDEX

Accra, 9
Adam, Karl, 78, 79
Agreed Syllabus, 40, 41
Altizer, T. J. J., 98, 99
Amis, Kingsley, 93
Anglican Church of Canada, 30
Anglican-Methodist Conversations, 9, 58, 88, 101–7, 108, 109, 110, 111, 113, 121
Anglican-Roman Catholic International Commission, (ARCIC), 86
Apostolic Ministry, The, 53, 54
Appeal to all Christian People, 29, 30
Aquinas, Thomas, 84
Areas of Ecumenical Experiment, 101, 113, 114
Azariah, Bishop of Dornakal, 20

Baldwin, James, 69
Baptist Union, 12, 13, 14, 16, 19, 118, 119
Barrett, Kingsley, 102, 106
Barth, Karl, 33, 34, 52
Beaverbrook, Lord, 59
Bell, G. K. A., Bishop, 46, 58
Bermondsey, 1
Biblical Criticism, 15 51–5
Birmingham, 33, 106, 111, 112, 113, 118
Black Record, 38
Body, The, 52
Boer War, 11
Bonhoeffer, Dietrich, 34, 46, 95
Book of Common Prayer, 14, 15, 25, 26, 72
Braithwaite, R. B., 98
Brent, Bishop, 32
Bristol Sponsoring Body, 114
Britain Today and Tomorrow, 112
British Council of Churches, 39, 100, 117

Bultmann, Rudolf, 96, 97
Butler, Christopher, 89
Butler, R. A., 40

Calvin, John, 113
Cambridge, 36, 111
Caradon, Lord, 69
Carpenter, Bishop, 58
Catholicity, 54
Catholicity of Protestantism, The, 54
Christianity and Social Order, 39
Christian Atheism, 99
Churchill, Winston, 27
Church of Christ, 118, 120
Church of England, 11, 12, 13, 14, 16, 17, 25, 26, 27, 28, 30, 31, 40, 49, 55, 56, 57, 58, 77, 88, 89, 101–7, 108, 109, 110, 111, 114, 118, 119, 120, 121
Church of North India, 9, 108
Church of Scotland, 30, 58, 59, 109
Church of South India, 29, 37, 46, 47, 53, 60
Church Relations in England, 57, 58
Church Times, 16
Clayton, T. B., 22
Clifford, John, 18
Cockin, Bishop, 49
Confessional Church (Germany), 34, 63
Congregational Church, 12, 13, 16, 19, 113, 118, 119
Council of Trent, 75
Couturier, Paul, 74
Cox, Harvey, 97, 98, 99

Davidson, Randall, Archbishop, 16, 20, 24, 26, 27
De Chardin, Teilhard, 79
Dix, Gregory, 53, 54, 72
Dodd, C. H., 53
Dual System of Education, 17, 18, 40

Edinburgh Conference, (1910), 19, 20, 21, 29, 32, 33
Edward VII, 11
Edward VIII, 24
Eliot, T. S., 24, 54
Eminent Victorians, 24
Epistle to the Ephesians, 19
Essays and Addresses, 77
Evangelical Church of Germany, 44

Faith and Order (Conferences and Commission meetings):
  Accra (1974), 115, 116, 117
  Edinburgh (1937), 35, 44, 61, 62
  Lausanne (1927), 32
  Louvain (1971), 115, 117
  Lund (1952), 9, 61, 62, 64, 65, 101
  Montreal (1963), 66
  Nottingham (1964), 100, 101, 113, 122
Faith and Order Movement, 20, 32, 44, 51, 78
Faulhaber, Cardinal, 79
Fisher, Geoffrey, Archbishop, 55, 56, 59, 105
Flew, R. Newton, 52, 61
Foundations, 15
Fullness of Christ, The, 54

Geneva, 44
George V, 11
Gore, Charles, 15
Gospel of Christian Atheism, The, 99
Greet, Kenneth, 119
Gregory of Tours, 79
Grindelwald, 19

Halifax, Lord, 78
Hamilton, W., 98
Heidegger, Martin, 96
Henson, Hensley, 16, 25, 26
Hitler, Adolf, 33, 34, 35, 38, 46
Honest to God, 93, 94, 95, 97
Hooper, J. S. M., 46
Hromdka, Joseph, 63, 64
Hughes, Hugh Price, 16
Hume, Cardinal, 89
Huxtable, John, 118
Hymns and Songs, 110

Iona, 74

Jesus and his Church, 52
John XXIII, Pope, 68, 75, 80, 81, 82, 87

Kaunda, Kenneth, 69
Kennedy, John, 92
Kensit, John, 14
Kikuyu, East Africa, 20
King, Edward, Bishop, 14
King, Martin Luther, 68, 92
Kirk, Kenneth, Bishop, 53
Küng, Hans, 85

Lambeth Conferences, 28, 29, 30
Lang, Archbishop, 24, 27
Lausanne, 32
Léger, Paul-Emile, 67
Leo XIII, Pope, 77
Letters from Prison, 95
Liberal Theology, 33, 76
Lidgett, John Scott, 17, 18, 19, 31
Life and Liberty Movement, 25, 110
Life and Work Conferences, 33, 35, 44, 46
Life and Work Movement, 32, 44
Lilje, Hans, 34, 46, 49
Liturgical Reform, 9, 71, 72, 73, 86, 110
Lloyd George, David, 11
Loisy, Alfred, 77
Lunn, Henry, 18
Luther, Martin, 34, 85
Lux Mundi, 15

MacLeod, George, 74
Macmillan, Harold, 91
Madras, 46
Malvern Conference (1941), 39
Manson, T. W., 54
Martin, Hugh, 36
Maurice, F. D., 16, 17
Mercier, Cardinal, 78
Methodist Church, 9, 11, 13, 19, 31, 32, 49, 58, 72, 73, 101-7, 108, 109, 110, 111, 115, 120
Methodist Church Act (1976), 110
Methodist Service Book, 110
Methodist Times, 16
Mitchell, Rosslyn, 26
Moltmann, Jürgen, 116
Morant, Robert, 18
Moravian Church, 118
Mortalium Animos, 78
Morton, Harry, 112

Mott, John R., 20
Müller, Ludwig, 35
Mystical Element of Religion, The, 77
Myth of God Incarnate, The, 15, 124

Nagpur, 109
New Theology, The, 15
Niemöller, Martin, 34, 45
Niles, Daniel T., 45
Nottingham Faith and Order Conference (1964), 100, 101, 113, 122

Observer, The, 94
Oldham, J. H., 20
On being a Christian, 85
Ordination of Women, 85, 111
Orthodox Churches, 44, 45, 61, 86
Oxford, 28, 36, 50

Paul VI, Pope, 85
Phenomenon of Man, 79
Pius IX, Pope, 76
Pius XI, Pope, 78
Pius XII, Pope, 72, 79
Political Theology, 100
Potter, Philip, 118
Prayer Book revision, 15, 25, 26, 72
Presbyterian Church, 13, 19, 58, 113
Primitive Church, The, 52
Primitive Methodism, 12, 13, 31
Programme to Combat Racism, 69, 118

Queen's College, Birmingham, 111

Radical Theologians, 99
Rahner, Karl, 84
Ramsey, Michael, 105, 106
Roberts, Harold, 58, 103
Robinson, John, 93, 94, 97, 99
Rodger, Patrick, 118
Roman Catholic Church, 12, 31, 32, 61, 66, 68, 71, 75–90, 103, 106, 112, 115, 119
Roman Catholic-Methodist Statements, 87
Russell, Bertrand, 24

Salvation Army, 11
Schlink, Edmund, 63, 64
Schutz, Roger, 73
Scottish Daily Express, 59
Scottish Episcopal Church, 58

Secular City, The, 97, 98
Secular Meaning of the Gospel, The, 97
Secular Theologians, 97, 98, 99
Shakespeare, J. H., 19
Shape of the Liturgy, The, 72
Shaw, Bernard, 24
Sheppard, H. R. L., 25
Söderblom, Nathan, 32
Stockholm, 33, 46
Stopford, Robert, 103
Strachey, Lytton, 24
Streeter, B. H., 15
Studdert-Kennedy, G. A., 22
Student Christian Movement, 20, 36, 50
Stuttgart, 44, 45
Syllabus of Errors, 76

Taizé, France, 73, 74
Temple, William, 15, 20, 25, 27, 32, 33, 36, 39, 41, 46, 60
Ten Propositions, 119, 120
Third World, 61, 68, 69, 116, 118
T'Hooft, Visser, 46
Thurian, Max, 73
Tillich, Paul, 95, 96
Tomkins, Oliver, 62
Torrance, T. F., 62
Tranquebar, India, 29
Tübingen, Germany, 35, 78, 85
Tynan, Kenneth, 93

United Church of Canada, 30, 31
United Methodist Church, 31
United Reformed Church, 113, 115, 118, 120
Uniting Church of Australia, 108

Van Buren, Paul, 97, 99
Vansittart, Robert, 38
Vatican I, 76
Vatican II, 68, 80, 81, 82, 83, 84, 85, 86, 90
Victoria, Queen, 11
Von Hügel, Friedrich, 77

Ward, Barbara, 69
Webb, Pauline, 69
Wells, H. G., 24
Wesleyan Methodist Church, 13, 14, 16, 19, 31
What is Christianity? 15
Woolf, Virginia, 24

131

World Council of Churches:
  Amsterdam Assembly (1948), 45, 65
  Evanston Assembly (1954), 64
  Nairobi Assembly (1975), 117, 118
  New Delhi Assembly (1961), 65, 70

Uppsala Assembly (1968), 9, 67, 68, 69, 70, 93, 100, 115, 117, 118
World War I, 21, 22
World War II, 38, 44, 48
Wurm, Bishop, 35

www.ingramcontent.com/pod-product-compliance
Lightning Source LLC
Chambersburg PA
CBHW050834160426
43192CB00010B/2023